QUEEN & COUNTRY™

BASTARDS.

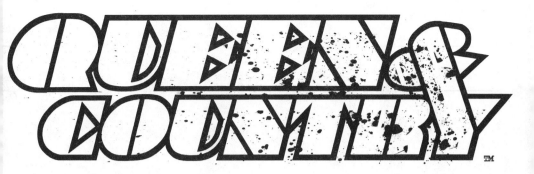

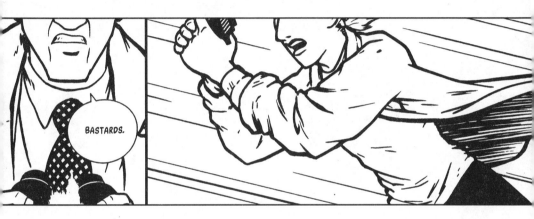

SCRIPTBOOK

by
Greg Rucka

featuring illustrations and
development material by
Steve Rolston

additional illustrations by
Tim Sale
Brian Hurtt
Leandro Fernandez

book design by
Laurenn McCubbin

edited by
James Lucas Jones

original series edited by
Jamie S. Rich

Published by Oni Press, Inc.

Joe Nozemack,
publisher

James Lucas Jones,
senior editor

Randal C. Jarrell,
managing editor

Original Queen & Country logo designed by Steven Birch @ Servo.

ONI PRESS, INC.
6336 SE Milwaukie Avenue,
PMB30
Portland, OR 97202
USA

www.onipress.com

First edition: June 2004
ISBN 1-929998-92-9

1 3 5 7 9 10 8 6 4 2
PRINTED IN CANADA.

This collects the scripts from issues 1-4 of the Oni Press comics series Queen & Country.

Queen & Country Issue One

Page 1

ONE:
Wide, big shot, establishing the OPS ROOM at midnight.[1]

We're looking from the back wall at the front of the room, slight down angle. This should be something like a cross between the Ops. Room from *The Sandbaggers*[2] and the Ops. Room used in *Patriot Games*[3] during the SAS raid on the training compound in Libya. Well lit, a lot of cigarette smoke hanging in the air. Computers, communications equipment. A couple STAFF who never speak, but are constantly moving back and forth.

We can see TWO MAIN DESKS/POSTS set up, including one on a slightly raised platform for the DUTY OPERATIONS OFFICER, currently staffed by a SMALL WHITE GUY in his early thirties named RON. RON is dressed in a suit, the coat off, his sleeves rolled up, but still in his tie. He has a headset on, a cigarette going in one hand, is drinking from a cup of coffee in the other, all the while talking on the net.

Seated near RON, leaning back in his chair, cigarette in his mouth, is WALLACE—head of the Special Section, late thirties, white, fit, dressed in a cheap suit. Eyes are closed.

A WOMAN IN HER LATE 20's named ALEXIS is seated at the MISSION DESK, or more appropriately, practically surrounded by it, since the desk is a horseshoe shape around where she is seated. ALEXIS, too, wears a headset, and is professionally dressed—slacks, blazer, blouse. At the desk is a computer terminal on which she is typing. A couple maps are spread out on the surface of the desk at her elbow.

On the far wall is a giant computer/display screen, kinda like the one they have to monitor the Space Shuttle launches at Mission Control, except more high-tech. This is the centerpiece of the room, and should be an impressive piece of hardware—we'll be coming back to this screen time and again throughout the series. [*If you want reference, I'd suggest watching* Patriot Games—*specifically the sequence where the SAS takes out the IRA training camp in Libya; also the beginning*

1 This is a huge panel description, as far as I'm concerned. Normally, I try to keep my panel descriptions to a paragraph or two, mostly for clarity's sake—though I'm sure there are editors and artists out there who would disagree with that assertion. In this case, I was after something very specific, which was not just the physical set, but the atmosphere of the set, as well. The sense of tension, of professionalism, of secrecy and even intimacy, were all elements I wanted thrown at the reader as soon as they hit the page. Part of the job of a First Issue, after all, is to define the world, and to entice the reader into following you further inside. So the Ops Room, as that point of entry, was pretty damn critical. Steve nailed it; he nailed it to such an extent that every artist to follow him—including Brian Hurtt in the Declassified series, which technically takes place some 20 years prior to this story—used (and continued to use) his floorplan. The details change, but the essence of Steve's Ops Room remains.

2 I can never say this enough: without The Sandbaggers, there would be no Queen & Country. I was sixteen, bookish, shy, and spent far too much time watching PBS (KTEH Channel 54 out of San Jose, California, for the record), and somehow, someway, I saw this amazing piece of dramatic television. Most of the shows I was in love with when I was sixteen, they don't hold up. The Sandbaggers, dated though it now is, does. And it was brilliant. Created by the late Ian Mackintosh, the show ran initially on ITV from 1978 to 1980, and is now available on DVD. Everyone should watch it. For more information on the show, including some great trivia, insight, and analysis of "the best damn drama you never saw," go to www.opsroom.org.

3 Contrary to rumor, I can't stand the work of Tom Clancy. But some of those films, they sure are pretty.

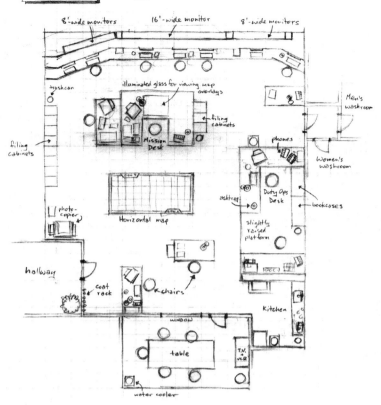

OPS ROOM

☐ — 2 feet × 2 feet

8'-wide monitors

16'-wide monitor

8'-wide monitors

trashcan

illuminated glass for viewing map overlays

Men's washroom

filing cabinets

filing cabinets

Mission Desk

phones

Women's washroom

filing cabinets

Horizontal map

ashtray

Duty Ops Desk

bookcases

slightly raised platform

photo-copier

hallway

coat rack

chairs

kitchen

WINDOW

table

T.V. & VCR

water cooler

4 I don't know why I started doing this, but somewhere in the course of writing for comics, I began adding these 'asides,' for lack of a better word, most often directed at the artist, but sometimes at the editor, or letter, or colorist.

of *Tomorrow Never Dies, when Bond is scoping the arms bazaar.*][4]

Currently the display shows a MAP OF THE WORLD, with time zones appropriately noted. Only TWO ZONES are key—Over the UK, one reads "0403 LOCAL (GMT)"; and over KOSOVO, another reads "0503 (Z)".

Also over Kosovo, we can see a marker of some sort on the map, either an icon of a flag or a dot or something—this should be over the city of PRIZREN. PRISTINA should also be marked on the map, though not highlighted. There's a call-out on PRIZREN, with a notation that is too small for us to read at this point.

Finally, in the center of the room, back to us and staring at the map, is Director of Operations PAUL CROCKER. Crocker's in his early 40's, wears a three-piece suit, smokes like a chimney, and if we were casting parts, would look like Robert Carslyle.

Everyone looks like they need some sleep.

1 TAILLESS/elec/small:
                    …standing by…

OPS room by Steve Rolston. *Q&C* Issue 1

2 CROCKER:

        Can we reach her?

3 RON:

        Yes, sir, she's on SHORT lead, via
        the Istanbul Number Two, call sign
        RAVEN.

4 RON/linked:

        He's on a sat-link to her, call
        sign CROW. She's in position…

TWO:
Zooming in on the map, now, OTS CROCKER, and we
see the callout for KOSOVO and PRIZREN. The CLOCK
now reads "0504 Z."

The callout reads:

        OPERATION: BROKEN GROUND_

5 RON:

        …been there ALL night.

6 CROCKER:

        Must be bloody FREEZING.

7 RON:

        Yes, sir.

OPS room by Brian Hurtt & Christine Norrie,
Q&C Issue 6

OPS room by Leandro Fernandez, *Q&C* Issue 8

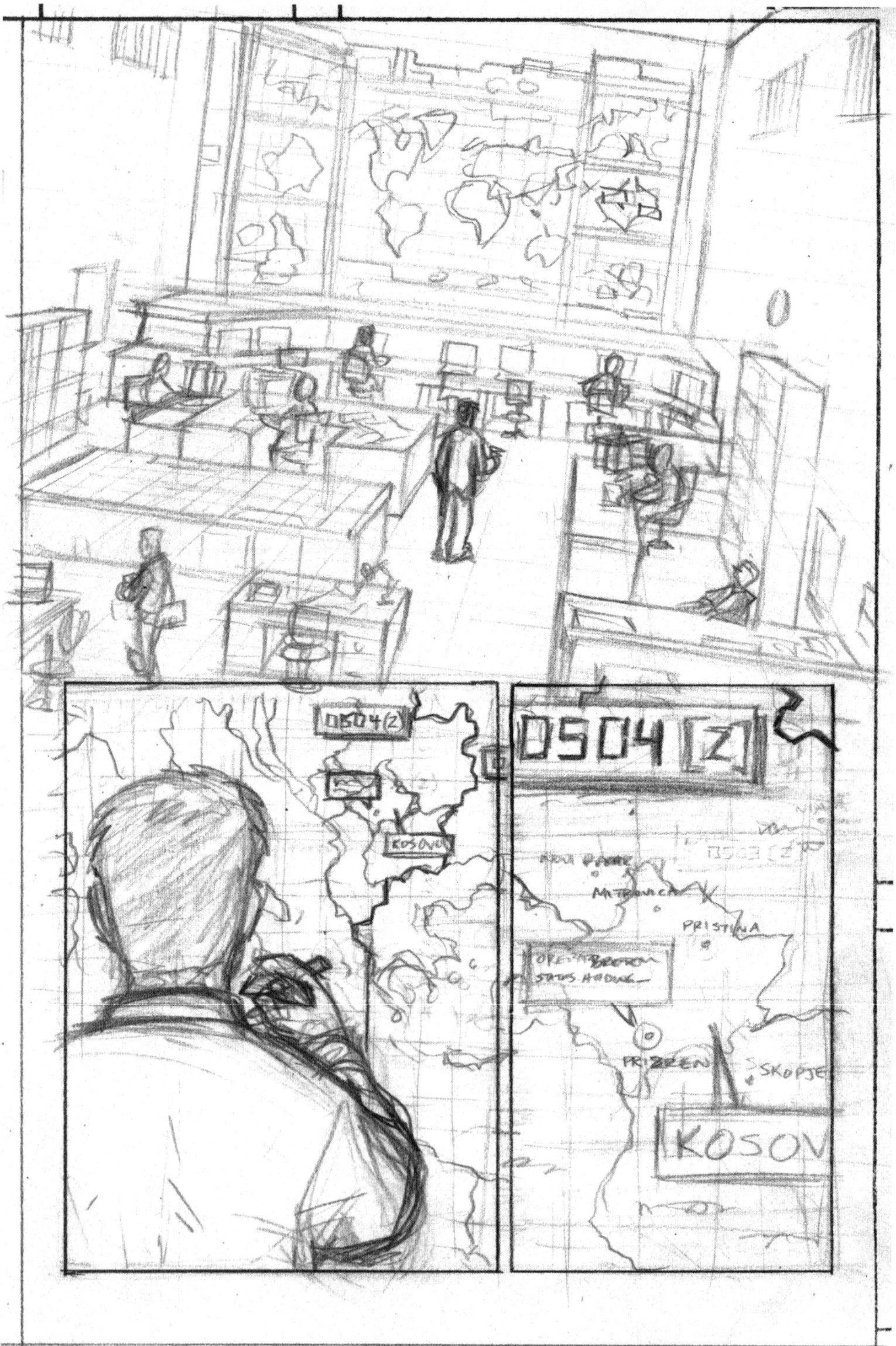
0504 [Z]
PRIZREN
SKOPJE
KOSOV

8 TAILLESS/elec/small:
                    —entering Prizren now.

THREE:
This is the completion of the zoom on the map,
we're centered on KOSOVO, can see that the country
is appropriately marked on the map. We can see
that PRIZREN is also marked.

The callout now reads:

                    OPERATION: BROKEN GROUND
                    STATUS: HOLDING_

9 CROCKER/off:
                    Lex, when's SUNRISE in ZONE?

Page 2

ONE:
Angle from the front, past ALEXIS at her desk,
looking at CROCKER. RON is partially in panel
at his desk. WALLACE has risen and is standing,
looking at CROCKER'S back. Everyone's expression
is very serious—they're talking life-or-death
shit, here.

1 ALEXIS:
                    Oh-five-seventeen, sir.

2 WALLACE:
                    Are we ABORTING?

TWO:
ECU CROCKER, scowling as he tips his head,
lighting a cigarette. WALLACE is coming closer in
background.

3 WALLACE:
                    Paul?

THREE:
Angle looking past CROCKER in FG, WALLACE right
behind him, over his shoulder. Each of them is
wearing concern, but for different reasons—Wallace
is worried about his number two, and Crocker is
worried about the fallout of the operation and
everything that can go wrong.

4 CROCKER:
                    SUNLIGHT hits her position, she'll
                    be BLOWN.

5 WALLACE:
                    She'll be BLOWN as soon as she
                    pulls the TRIGGER.

6 WALLACE/linked:

> The QUESTION is can she get out in
> TIME?

FOUR:
CU CROCKER, having pivoted about halfway to face
WALLACE. CROCKER looks pissy, scowling. WALLACE
looks attentive, and still obviously tense.

7 CROCKER:

> The question is CAN she HIT the
> target?

8 WALLACE:

> You KNOW she can, Boss...

FIVE:
Angle past WALLACE in FG, turning to look at
CROCKER, who is now leaning on the D.O.O.'s desk,
directing his speech to RON. RON has one hand to
his headset, checking.

9 WALLACE:

> ...it's why you sent HER and not
> me.

10 CROCKER:

> What's Markovsky's ETA?

11 RON:

> Checking, sir.

SIX:
Narrow panel, wide shot of the room from the back.
RON is checking for an answer, ALEXIS is busy at
her desk.

WALLACE and CROCKER are both looking at the map,
or more specifically, the clock over Kosovo.

12 CROCKER:

> Well HURRY it up.

SEVEN:
ECU KOSOVO CLOCK.

Now reading:

0507 Z

NO COPY.

Page 3

ONE:
Angle past ALEXIS in FG, one hand on her headset. She's looking to CROCKER, who has turned, still scowling, cigarette dangling from his lips.

RON is still busily doing his thing.

WALLACE is lighting himself another cigarette.

1 ALEXIS:

        Sir? RAVEN is asking for INSTRUCTIONS.

2 CROCKER: Tell him to bloody well wait. It's not his ASS in the NEST, is it?

TWO:
OTS CROCKER, looking at WALLACE, whose expression is something between incredulity and frustration.

3 CROCKER:

        She gets CAUGHT, the Foreign Office'll EAT me for DINNER.

4 WALLACE:

        DON'T tell me you didn't CLEAR the RUN?

THREE:
From the map, CROCKER looking at the clock, off. RON is addressing his back.

5 CROCKER:

        I couldn't risk Weldon saying NO.

6 RON:

        It's CONFIRMED, sir. Markovsky came in over the Macedonian border twenty-three minutes ago, through the German sector.

FOUR:
CROCKER looking at WALLACE. Both of them know what this means, neither of them look particularly happy.

7 WALLACE/small:

        Well, that's THAT, then, isn't it?

FIVE:
Angle past ALEXIS as CROCKER addresses her. The scowl is gone. He's made his decision.

8 CROCKER:

        Lex, order to RAVEN from D. Ops. Tell him CROW is free to FLY.

9 ALEXIS:
                    Yes, sir.

SIX:
CU of the map, KOSOVO section again, the call-out.
Now reads:

                    OPERATION: BROKEN GROUND
                    STATUS: FREE RUN

10 ALEXIS/off:
                    M.C.O.   for   Raven,   orders   as
                    follow:
11 ALEXIS/linked/off:
                    From   Director   Operations   Paul
                    Crocker…

Page 4

ONE:
This is gonna be kinda tricky, so I apologize in
advance.

We're looking straight on at TARA CHACE[5][6]. She is
prone, in a sniper's nest, sheltered by rubble.
She's on the fifth floor of a bombed-out building,
sighting through a shattered wall. Broken
concrete and masonry, including exposed rebar,
are providing shelter.

It's dawn, and a light dusting of snow covers her
position.

She is settled behind an Accuracy International
AWP sniper's rifle with a pretty big scope on it
mounted on a bipod [*Steve—I've got reference for
this if you want it.*][7]. Beside her is a TWO-WAY
RADIO set, and a pair of HIGH-POWER BINOCULARS, on
a short tripod. All the equipment is camouflaged.

CHACE is wearing a Ghillie suit, with a sniper's
cowl—basically a very fine weave camo net—pulled
over her head and draped around her shoulders.

The effect we're going for is that everything
is almost merging with the background because of
camouflage. CHACE herself should be very hard to
spot.

1 CAPTION:
                    "…Crow is free to fly…."

2 CAPTION/Chace:
                    The last time I was this COLD I was
                    at the South Pole.[8]

TWO:
CU CHACE, settling herself behind the scope. Her
hair is tied back. She looks determined.

5 Tara Felicity Chace is a lovely young lady who now lives in Seattle and speaks something like forty-seven languages, and works as a professional translator. She and I went to high school together. She and I would stay up late and sit on the floor in the darkened living room of her parents' home in Monterey, and we would watch video tapes of spy stories—mostly Sir Alec Guinness as George Smiley in Smiley's People and Tinker, Tailor, Soldier, Spy, The Sandbaggers, and, if I remember correctly, The Prisoner. We were adolescents with bubbling hormones, and we'd sneak out in the middle of the night and watch spy stories together. Tell me that's not seriously fucked up. I mean, I don't think we even ever kissed. And we did this a lot. I look back on it, and I suspect we were probably madly in love with one another, and too dumb to realize it (well, at least I was), and I know that she was my best friend in the whole wide world then. But it was high school and there was adolescent bullshit, and I never told her that. So I'm telling her that now.
And that's why Tara Chace is named Tara Chace.

6 Normally, when introducing a new character, I give a paragraph of description, as I did for Crocker back on script-page 1; here I didn't, simply because Steve had been faxing me sketches of Chace for months, and I'd been sending them back with notes like 'more like this' and 'no, no, icky,' and 'yes!!!'

7 He didn't.

3 CAPTION/Chace:

           Why doesn't Crocker EVER send me somewhere HOT?

THREE:
POV CHACE, through the scope, and we're seeing the wreckage of Prizren, a large open area of what was once an intersection on the main road. Buildings are in various stages of collapse and rubble—Prizren took it pretty bad during the war. At the same time, some obvious repair work has been done, and the city has signs of life and, even, normalcy.

At the intersection is a parked 3 TON TRUCK, with three KLA irregulars loafing nearby. They're joking with one another, smoking cigarettes. All have AK-47s slung over shoulders or across their backs.

Sunlight is starting to lance through gaps in the surrounding buildings.

Across the intersection, some crumpled NEWSPAPER is blowing from right to left.

4 CAPTION/Chace:

           Need to COMPENSATE for the WIND....

5 CAPTION/Chace:

           ...maybe he won't SHOW....

FOUR:
Angle from the intersection, as another TRUCK, this one much older, rattles into the intersection opposite the 3 TON TRUCK.

KLA GUYS are moving to greet.

In EBG we can see CHACE'S BUILDING, where her sniper's nest is. Sunlight is creeping up the front of the building. We should not be able to actually see Chace.

NO COPY.

8. Ah, this got me into so much trouble. There's been much speculation that Tara Chace is actually the character Lily Sharpe, who I wrote about in Whiteout. At the start—and I mean waaaay back at the start—when I first began discussing with Jamie (S. Rich) and Joe (Nozemack) the possibility of doing an ongoing spy series for Oni, Lily seemed the logical character to use; she'd appeared once before in an Oni series, I liked her, and it seemed logical enough. It was my intent to actually use Lily...until I actually began jotting notes down for the series. I write biographies (short ones!) for my main characters whenever I start a project; I'd known I was going to use the name Tara Chace (see note 5), so that was the name I used in the bio...and as I wrote it, as the character began to take shape, she kept moving further and further from Lily, until ultimately, I had to acknowledge I had a completely different character on my hands. I kept the line through rewrites, partially as an Easter Egg to those folks who had read Whiteout, partially as a joke. If I'd had a brain in my head, though, I wouldn't have done it at all, because it's lead to all sorts of aggravation and general headaches with rights people and the like, none of which is really worth going into here. Corner me at the bar at some convention and fill me with good scotch, I'll give you the story then. But it'll take a lot of scotch, I'm warning you now, and I like the expensive stuff.

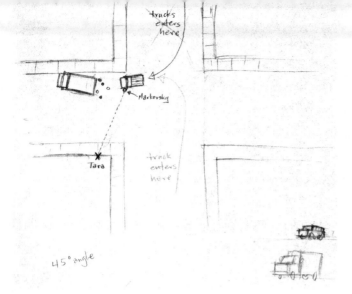

Page 5

ONE:
POV CHACE, through the scope. The OLD TRUCK has stopped about fifteen feet away from the back of the 3 TON TRUCK. TWO RUSSIAN MAFIA TYPES are coming out of the new truck, moving to greet the 3 KLA SOLDIERS.

1 CAPTION/Chace:
             Dammit...

TWO:
OTS MARKOVSKY, still in the cab of the OLD TRUCK. Past him, over the hood, we can see the TWO RUSSIAN MAFIA TYPES walking to the back of the 3 TON TRUCK, escorted by ONE of the KLA SOLDIERS.

MARKOVSKY, for the record, is an entirely ordinary looking Russian in his late forties.

2 CAPTION/Chace:
             ...get OUT of the TRUCK, General.

THREE:
Angle past the TWO RUSSIAN MAFIA TYPES.

A KLA SOLDIER has pulled back the tarp covering the rear of the 3 TON TRUCK, revealing, inside, LOTS OF GUNS. We're talking rifles, pistols, heavy machine guns, some of it in crates, some of it loose. A small MORTAR rests in the middle of everything.[9]

3 CAPTION/Chace:
             INSPECT the merchandise, do SOMETHING...

FOUR:
POV CHACE, angle on the cab of the OLD TRUCK. We

[9] I do a lot of research. I try to use multiple sources. When I veer from reality, I tend to do so for one of two reasons—either because it's dramatically necessary, or because the reality is so convoluted and complicated that there's no hope of making it clear in a 24 page issue. The scenario being described above—with the exception of the CIA sanctioned assassination that Tara is about to commit—is entirely real. Throughout the late '90s, the KLA was buying and selling arms like nobody's business on the black market, rather than surrendering them to NATO, as they were supposed to be doing. My interest in the subject came from reading an editorial in the British Medical Journal, from August 14, 1999, and then an article in the Hindustan Times, from Tuesday, August 17, 1999. Yes, I have strange reading habits. Incidentally, I've had it confirmed by someone who was actually in Kosovo at the time that the trade described above happened with alarming frequency.

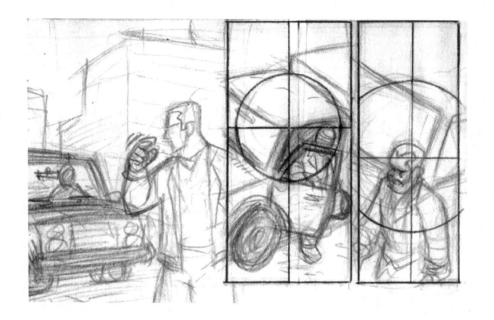

can't see MARKOVSKY, only his slight shadow.

4 CAPTION/Chace: …give me a SHOT.

FIVE:
Angle past ONE of the RUSSIAN MAFIA TYPES, who has turned and is beckoning to MARKOVSKY in the cab of the OLD TRUCK.

5 CAPTION/Chace:
                    There you GO, they've brought the
                    GUNS, now give the nice soldiers
                    their MONEY…

SIX:
POV CHACE, through the scope, the cab of the OLD TRUCK, as MARKOVSKY steps out. He's carrying a DUFFEL BAG.

6 CAPTION/Chace:
                    Good…good…

7 CAPTION/Chace:
                    …inhale…

SEVEN:
POV CHACE, through the scope, as the crosshairs come to rest on MARKOVSKY'S head.

8 CAPTION/Chace: …exhale…

9 CAPTION/Chace: …hold…

10 CAPTION/Chace: …and…

Page 6

ONE:
Closer, angle as MARKOVSKY'S head is blown open by
a .308 magnum round. The round has passed through
Markovsky and has shattered the WINDOW on the OLD
TRUCK.[10]

NO COPY.

TWO:
CU as MARKOVSKY slumps down the side of the trunk.
The side of his head facing away from Chace's
position is literally almost half gone—a .308 is
a big round. The WINDOW has shattered, and blood,
brain, and bone are misting the inside of the
cab.

NO COPY.

THREE:
MARKOVSKY toppling to the ground, the KLA SOLDIERS
and the RUSSIAN MAFIA TYPES all staring in shock,
just now beginning to move.

MARKOVSKY has dropped the duffel.

NO COPY.

FOUR:
Smaller, narrow panel. CU CHACE, looking directly
at her over the barrel of the rifle, as she comes
off the sight. She's pulling the cowl down with
one hand, revealing her features.

Her expression is grim. She's not proud of what
she just did.

NO COPY.

10 Like the Ops Room on page 1, I
wanted the violence here to be sharp,
shocking, and realistic; in short, I wanted
it to set the tone for the rest of the
series—that bullets were very bad things
and that people died, and they died
quickly, and horribly, and rarely with
the luxury of seeing it coming. This is
one of those places where the panel
descriptions really means nothing, it's all
up to the artist. Steve did a brilliant job
here, in my view, conveying not only the
horror of the murder, but the shock of it,
as well.

Page 7

ONE:
View of the intersection, and now the KLA SOLDIERS
and the RUSSIAN MAFIA TYPES all diving for
cover.

NO COPY.[11]

TWO:
Angle from behind the KLA SOLDIERS, behind cover,
their weapons out. The LEAD KLA GUY speaking on
a RADIO. Whatever it is he's saying, he's pretty
damn upset.

The OTHER TWO are firing on Chase's position,
off.

11 I use these silent panels a lot when I
write comics. There are readers out there
who think that makes me lazy. They're
stupid and should go read books with lots
of big sound effects, and leave me alone.
I use NO COPY panels for a number
of reasons, but primarily because what
I write is only half—if that—of what a
comic book is. The art is as crucial as any
word, as any sound effect.
For this sequence, sound effects seemed
to me to be entirely inappropriate;
rather than filling the panels with word
balloons of half-completed exclamations,
it seemed far more elegant and powerful
to drop into a complete silence, and let
Steve's pencils provide the sound.

(NO BG)

NO COPY.

THREE:
Angle past the OLD TRUCK, as the KLA LEADER, still
yelling on his radio, is motioning the OTHER TWO
after him as he heads for the building.

NO COPY.

FOUR:
Angle from the exterior, but closer, on the nest.
No sign of Chace. BULLETS are tearing hell out of
the remaining masonry, ricocheting off brick.

The RIFLE, RADIO, and BINOCULARS are all still in
place. Chace herself is gone.

Lots of bullets hitting the position.

NO COPY.

FIVE:
Wide, extreme longshot of the intersection.
The KLA SOLDIERS are now advancing on CHACE'S
BUILDING, the RUSSIA MAFIA TYPES now crouched
around MARKOVSKY'S BODY.

This is pretty much a big tableau, still-life
almost.

NO COPY.

SIX:
CU of the SUN rising over the buildings in the
east. It is now officially daylight.

NO COPY.

Page 8

ONE:
Exterior of the building, this is the "back" of the
structure, the side away from the intersection.
Marginally more intact than the side that was
facing the intersection, previous.

CHACE is crouching in the broken doorway, swathed
in shadow, looking out. She's checking to see that
her route is clear across the street. She still
wears the Ghillie suit.

The SUN is still creeping higher, casting long
shadows up and down the block.

NO COPY.

TWO:
Shot along this new street, this can be about
knee-level or so, looking up slightly. The street

is peppered with broken rocks and bricks and glass.

CHACE is sprinting from the open doorway on our left, where her sniper's nest was, towards another building on the opposite side of the street. She's running across the pockets of daylight. The Ghillie suit makes her hard to see.

NO COPY.

THREE:
OTS KLA SOLDIER, in FG, as he comes around the back corner of Chace's building, turning right. He is looking to his right, weapon ready. Looking nervous.

In EBG, we can see CHACE disappearing into the doorway of the building opposite the one she just left.

NO COPY.

FOUR:
Reverse of ONE.

CHACE is in her new doorway, pressing herself back into the shadows, looking back over her shoulder.

Past her, in BG, we can see TWO KLA SOLDIERS, one coming from either side of the building she just left. They're meeting in the doorway she just abandoned, looking around, preparing to go inside.

NO COPY.

FIVE:
POV CHACE, as the TWO KLA SOLDIERS enter the other building, covering one another as they disappear inside.

NO COPY.

SIX:
CU CHACE, her expression. Relief, but her eyes are still very wary. This is far from over.

NO COPY.

Page 9

ONE:
Interior of the new building. Lots of rubble, ruined furniture, more broken masonry.

CHACE is unzipping the Ghillie suit, pulling one arm free. She's wearing a flannel shirt over a turtleneck and heavy jeans beneath the suit.

NO COPY.

TWO:
Close on CHACE'S BOOTS as the Ghillie suit drops to the ground. Past it, we can see a shadow-filled gap behind some broken masonry.

NO COPY.

THREE:
Same angle as previous, but now CHACE is crouching, reaching into the hole.

NO COPY.

FOUR:
Same as previous, but CHACE has now pulled a BUNDLE from the hiding place.

NO COPY.

FIVE:
Same as previous, but now CHACE is stuffing the Ghillie suit into the hiding place.

NO COPY.

SIX:
CHACE crouching in FG, unwrapping the bundle, which we can now see is a JACKET.

NO COPY.

SEVEN:
CU CHACE'S BACK, pulling the jacket on. We can see a stencil, the UNITED NATIONS LOGO. Above it should be the words UNITED NATIONS or U.N. [*Steve-I can't find an actual reference for this jacket, but I'm reliably informed it exists in some form or other—probably doesn't say "United Nations" on it, but certainly would have the emblem.*][12]

NO COPY.

12 Doing this, of course, is entirely illegal and honestly, pretty skanky; but then again, the British bugged the Secretary General's Office at the U.N., so I suppose this pales in comparison.

Page 10

ONE:
Wide, narrow shot, of the street. CHACE has emerged from the building, in her U.N. JACKET, and is walking briskly away, making for the corner in the BG, right of panel.

In FG, turning the FG corner, left of panel, is KLA LEADER, reacting.

1 CAPTION/Chace:
　　　　　　And it was going so WELL...

TWO:
At the other corner, CHACE in FG, head down, pretending she doesn't hear. Her expression is scared, though.

In BG, coming from his corner, the KLA LEADER is running after her, raising his AK, shouting.

2 CAPTION/Chace:
                    ...don't need to SPEAK Croatian[13] to
                    know WHAT he's shouting.

13   I got this wrong. The KLA—the Kosovo Liberation Army—was/is comprised mostly of Kosovar Albanians; as such, they would either be shouting in Albanian, or, potentially, Serbian.

THREE:
OTS KLA LEADER, sighting with the AK at CHACE'S BACK, as she reaches the corner.

NO COPY.

FOUR:
Angle, as CHACE ducks around the corner in FG. In BG the KLA LEADER is opening fire.

NO COPY.

FIVE:
Along the street that CHACE has just turned down, as she sprints towards us, away from the corner.

In BG, opposite the corner she turned, at an angle, we can see where the ROUNDS from the LEADER'S SHOTS are RICOCHETING off the rubble, and then bouncing crazily around the street—into the air, into the street, and some of them are dangerously close to CHASE.

NO COPY.

Page 11

ONE:
High angle, looking down from the end of the street. At the top of the panel, KLA LEADER has turned the corner, still shooting. He is being joined by the TWO OTHER SOLDIERS.

At the bottom of the panel, CHACE is running for her life.

NO COPY.

TWO:
Lower angle, CHASE sliding over the hood of a PARKED CAR.

In EBG, the SOLDIERS are pursuing her.

The neighborhood is getting somewhat better,

meaning less rubble, more repair.

1 CAPTION/Chace:
                    What is it Wallace always says?

THREE:
On the opposite side of the car, CHACE coming up
and running into an alley.

The KLA LEADER is reloading. The OTHER TWO are
still shooting, and doing a fair amount of damage
to the car.

RICOCHETS are bouncing around crazily, smashing
glass, burying themselves into brick and the
like.

2 CAPTION/Chace:
                    It's not the BULLET that has
                    your NAME on it you have to worry
                    about...

FOUR:
Shot of the entrance of the alley, at an angle.
CHACE'S head is moving out of panel, ducking.

BULLETS are ripping into the brick where her head
would have been, RICOCHETING.

3 CAPTION/Chace:
                    ...it's all those OTHER ones...

FIVE:
CU CHACE'S left calf, as one of the RICOCHETS[14]
punches through her pants leg.

4 CAPTION/Chace:
                    ...marked to WHOM it may CONCERN—[15]

SIX:
Angle on the street as CHACE tumbles from the hit,
going down, hard.

5 CAPTION/Chace:
                    ...bloody HELL...

SEVEN:
CU CHACE'S FACE, grimacing in pain as she rolls
onto her back on the ground.

6 CAPTION/Chace:
                    ...I DON'T want to DIE in Kosovo.

Page 12[16]

ONE:
ECU of an overflowing ashtray on the D.O.O.'s
desk, as WALLACE'S hand crushes out yet another
smoke. We can see just a fraction of RON past the
ashtray.

14 This was important to me—though
I suspect I was the only who cared; if
the bullet had struck Chace's leg dead
on, there was a good chance she could
have lost the leg. I wanted the wounds
to be as realistic as the violence in this
series, and thus, I had to burn off a lot of
the round's velocity before I could let the
bullet strike her. Hence the ricochet.

15 This line was stolen from my very
good friend Jerry Hennelly, who has
served as one of my main research
sources for several years, now. Jerry
currently works as a cop. He has served
in the Army, and worked as a Personal
Security Agent for several years. He
knows all sorts of things that fascinate
and frighten me. He's also a hell of a guy,
and a dear, dear friend. It was he who told
me this line over lunch in a restaurant in
New York several years ago, and I'd been
looking for a place to use it ever since
then.

16 There's a line by the late Douglas
Adams that was used in the second
series of the Hitchhiker's Guide to the
Galaxy radio series: "And since this is
of course an immensely frustrating and
nervewracking moment for the narrative
to suddenly switch tracks again, that is
precisely what the narrative will now do."
Which is another way to say, hey, look,
dramatic pacing.

1 RON:
> Sir? Just in from PRIZREN...

TWO:
In the OPS ROOM, angle past CROCKER as he turns to exchange looks with WALLACE. Not very happy.

RON is visible past WALLACE'S ELBOW, speaking to CROCKER.

2 RON:
> ...reports of GUNFIRE and a PURSUIT.

3 CROCKER:
> Anything ELSE?

4 RON:
> Yes, sir. One FATALITY, male.

THREE:
CROCKER and WALLACE, heads together.

5 CROCKER:
> So she got him before she was blown.

6 WALLACE:
> Is that going to help you SLEEP better when she doesn't come back?[17]

17 Wallace is Crocker's conscience. He's not saying anything that Crocker doesn't know, of course.

FOUR:
CROCKER crossing to the MONITOR WALL, focused on it. ALEXIS is snapping into action.

WALLACE stands still in BG, very concerned.

7 CROCKER: Lex, what's the EGRESS?

8 ALEXIS: Istanbul Number Two recruited DRIVER picks her up north of Prizren. Travel via U.N. vehicle, U.N. cover north to PRISTINA...

FIVE:
OTS CROCKER, looking at the MONITOR as it changes to a zoom of KOSOVO, showing the roadways from PRIZREN to PRISTINA. The map also marks the various sectors—PRISTINA is U.K., PRIZREN is GERMAN. Also shows the ITALIAN, FRENCH, and AMERICAN sectors.

9 ALEXIS/off: ...to the British Sector, where she meets our CONTACT and is FLOWN out of country.

10 CROCKER: If she misses the rendezvous? Is there a fall-back?

SIX:
OTS CROCKER, looking at ALEXIS. ALEXIS is sober.

11 ALEXIS:
> No, sir. She's on her own.

SEVEN:
OTS CROCKER, now taking in WALLACE and ALEXIS.

12 WALLACE:
> And UNARMED?

13 ALEXIS:
> Yes. She was to go WEAPONLESS[18] after the HIT, in case she was STOPPED at any of the CHECKPOINTS....

[18] This was another point I wanted to make clear in this issue, especially in light of the events in Issue Three; guns are a big deal. They create as many, if not more, problems than they solve; Tara trying to cross a border with a gun is a quick way to get arrested, for instance. Unlike James Bond, the Minders do not go armed unless absolutely necessary. There's an additional dramatic dividend, here; when the Minders are ordered to take up arms, it adds that much more tension to their situation. By establishing the respect and reluctance to use firearms, I was trying to give them the weight they deserve.

Page 13

ONE:
Wide of the OPS ROOM, everyone still, and in their same positions.

NO COPY.

TWO:
CROCKER turning back to WALLACE once more, putting a cigarette to his lips. RON, in BG, is answering one of the phones on his desk.

3 RON/small:
> Duty Ops. Officer...

4 CROCKER:
> Eighty-seven kilometers from PRIZREN to PRISTINA...

6 WALLACE:
> With KLA, NATO, and U.N. troops all along the way.

THREE:
Angle past RON, still on the phone. WALLACE is lighting CROCKER'S cigarette.

7 WALLACE:
> You going to notify the Foreign Office?

8 CROCKER:
> Not YET. She COULD still make it.

9 RON/small:
> Yes, sir, I'll tell him.

FOUR:
OTS RON, CROCKER reacting to the statement. CROCKER is angry as ever.

10 RON:
> Deputy Chief, sir. Wants you in his office right away.

FIVE:
Angle from the entrance of the OPS ROOM, CROCKER storming towards us, not happy at all. RON, WALLACE, and ALEXIS all looking after him.

11 CROCKER:
> Call me if there are any developments.

12 WALLACE:
> What're you going to tell Weldon?

SIX:
CROCKER, snarling.

13 CROCKER: Depends on how much he already KNOWS.

Page 14

ONE:
Back in Prizren, the alley.

CHACE is pulling herself upright using the side of a building. A DOORWAY is further along the alley.

1 CAPTION/Chace:
> First rule...

TWO:
Angle from the opposite end of the alley, as CHACE limps her way towards us, trailing blood from her wounded calve.

2 CAPTION/Chace:
> ...keep MOVING.[19]

19 Again, I didn't make this up, though I can't remember the source for them off the top of my head. Probably some declassified Army manual on Escape & Evasion tactics.

THREE:
CU CHACE'S expression, she's sweating, in pain, but her eyes are lighting up.

3 CAPTION/Chace:
> Second rule...

FOUR:
Slight down angle, overlooking a SQUARE filled with Albanian and Croatian WOMEN and children, all of them gathered around a WELL in its center. They are filling buckets with water, doing laundry, etc. These women are predominantly Muslim, and as such are dressed accordingly, heavy black cloaks, faces covered.

In BG, from the alley, CHACE is emerging, pulling

off her jacket.

In low FG, a TRUCK is parked, just inside panel.

4 CAPTION/Chace:
                ...find a CROWD.[19]

FIVE:
CHACE pushes through the crowd, trying to disappear
into it. The jacket is off and in her hands.

NO COPY.

SIX:
Angle from inside the alley, past the THREE KLA
SOLDIERS as they reach the end, looking out to see
the crowd of WOMEN around the WELL.

NO COPY.

Page 15

ONE:
Angle as the KLA LEADER gestures for his men
to disperse the crowd. The TWO KLA SOLDIERS are
trying to follow the orders, but the WOMEN aren't
moving.

NO COPY.

TWO:
KLA LEADER, with his AK in the air, opening fire.

NO COPY.

THREE:
OTS LEADER, as the WOMEN all scatter for cover,
grabbing their CHILDREN, abandoning their
buckets, terrified. LAUNDRY is left in piles on
the ground.

NO COPY.

FOUR:
POV KLA LEADER, looking at the pile of laundry,
the U.N. JACKET atop it, and a trail of blood
leading around the well.

NO COPY.

FIVE:
Angle, as the KLA LEADER follows the trail of
blood to the CAB OF THE PARKED TRUCK, motioning
the TWO SOLDIERS to cover him.

NO COPY.

SIX:
Close angle, KLA LEADER against the truck, AK
wedged to his hip, reaching for the door to the
cab of the truck. The TWO SOLDIERS are sighting
on the cab.

NO COPY.

<u>SEVEN:</u>
KLA LEADER yanks the door open.

NO COPY.

<u>EIGHT:</u>
OTS KLA LEADER, looking at the empty cab.

NO COPY.

Page 16

<u>ONE:</u>
Back in London, interior of WELDON'S OFFICE, which
is a nicely appointed room, a little cramped, with
a large desk and several filing cabinets. A couple
paintings on the walls. A computer on the desk.

WELDON, in his late forties, kind of a Bob Hoskins
type, is in a suit, sipping a cup of tea behind
his desk.

CROCKER has just entered the office, one hand still
on the door.

Sunlight is edging through the windows.

1 WELDON:
            Paul. Hope I didn't DISTURB you.

2 CROCKER:
            I was in the Ops. Room.

3 WELDON:
            Yes, I KNOW...

<u>TWO:</u>
OTS CROCKER as he moves to the desk, opposite
WELDON. WELDON is leaning back in his chair,
holding his cup of tea in both hands. He's looking
like he doesn't take shit from anyone, least of
all Crocker.

4 WELDON:
            ...what I DON'T know is why Tara
            Chace is in Kosovo.

5 CROCKER:
            Is she?

6 WELDON:
            You DAMN well KNOW she IS!

<u>THREE:</u>
Angle as WELDON leans forward, snarling. CROCKER
doesn't move.

7 WELDON:

>   You're running a SPECIAL operation
>   in KOSOVO and I want to know WHY!

8 WELDON/linked:

>   What the hell is Broken Ground?

FOUR:
OTS WELDON, CROCKER'S expression, mouth shut, almost contemptuous.

9 WELDON:

>   I want an ANSWER, Paul!

FIVE:
OTS WELDON, CROCKER'S expression, considering what to say.

NO COPY.

SIX:
CROCKER, relenting.

10 CROCKER:

>   It's a FAVOR to the CIA. Former
>   Russian General, Igor Grigorivich
>   Markovsky.

SEVEN:
WELDON, still suspicious, again sipping his tea. CROCKER is still standing, not relaxed, but not as confrontational.

11 WELDON:

>   He's retired, Markovsky.

12 CROCKER:

>   He's Russian MOB, buying GUNS from
>   the KLA and then selling them to
>   the CHECHENS.

Page 17

ONE:
OTS WELDON, at CROCKER.

1 CROCKER:

>   CIA asked if we could put a STOP to
>   it.

TWO:
WELDON, setting his cup of tea down very carefully on his desk. He's furious. He's not looking at Crocker.

2 WELDON:

>   You used one of Her Majesty's
>   agents to commit MURDER at the
>   American's behest?

THREE:
CROCKER, unrepentant.

3 CROCKER:

>   Not for FREE.

4 CROCKER/linked:

>   In exchange we get KEYHOLE[20] support
>   and analysis for OUR operations in
>   North Africa and Asia.

FOUR:
WELDON, rising, both hands on the desk, still just
livid with CROCKER. CROCKER is, paradoxically, the
most relaxed we've seen him—he's almost smiling.

5 CROCKER:

>   That's INTELLIGENCE we couldn't
>   get otherwise—

6 WELDON:

>   That HARDLY justifies you mounting
>   an UNAUTHORIZED assassination!

FIVE:
OTS WELDON, CROCKER, sincere.

7 CROCKER:

>   I think it DOES. The CIA does
>   favors for US all the time.

8 CROCKER/linked:

>   Now they owe me—

9 WELDON: YOU?

SIX:
CU CROCKER, bare smile.

10 CROCKER: Us.
11 CROCKER/linked:

>   Now they owe US. It's GOOD for the
>   Service, sir.

SEVEN:
WELDON, fuming.

NO COPY.

EIGHT:
WELDON, picking up his tea once more, the kind
of fury that makes you whisper instead of shout.
CROCKER is turning to go.

12 WELDON: I HOPE that'll be CONSOLATION for
>   Chace's FAMILY.

13 CROCKER: I doubt it, Sir.

NINE:
CU CROCKER.

14 CROCKER: She doesn't HAVE any.[21]

ONE:
OTS CHACE, looking out a cracked window at a street in Prizren. A HUMVEE is rolling down the street, U.N. Peacekeepers atop it. It's passing a parked car.

CHACE is wearing the black robe the Muslim women were wearing.

1 CAPTION/Chace:
                    Blown the rendezvous to HELL.

TWO:
Reveal that CHACE is in an empty bedroom, a little bed in a corner. The place looks like it was abandoned in a hurry. She's sitting on the bed, her left knee up, her foot on the bed with her. She's rolled the pant's leg up. There's a lot of blood.

2 CAPTION/Chace:
                    Crocker must be APOPLECTIC.

THREE:
CHACE, taking a corner of the black cloak between her teeth and tearing a strip free.

3 CAPTION/Chace:
                    Weldon's got to know by now, too.

FOUR:
CHACE tying the strip of fabric tightly around the wound in her calf. For the record, it's a flesh wound. Most of the bullet was spent when it hit her.

4 CAPTION/Chace: Wonder who won THAT fight.

FIVE:
CHACE rolling her pant leg back down.

5 CAPTION/Chace:
                    Lucky it was only a RICOCHET that
                    hit me.
6 CAPTION/Chace:
                    Hurts like HELL all the SAME.

SIX:
OTS CHACE, again looking out the window.

The HUMVEE is gone, but the parked car remains on the street. SOLDIERS are patrolling nearby.

7 CAPTION/Chace: Time to GO.

Page 19

ONE:
Exterior street, the SOLDIERS are on patrol. Civilians in various garb are out and about, too. Some are being questioned by the PEACEKEEPERS.

CHACE is crossing the street, wrapped in the black cloak, making for the car.

It's about 10:30 local time, now, the SUN is high. Puddles on the street from melted snow.

NO COPY.

TWO:
Angle past a PEACEKEEPER in FG, who has turned from the MAN he is questioning to watch CHACE as she reaches the car.

1 CAPTION/Chace:
            Too much to HOPE that the KEYS are
            in.

THREE:
POV CHACE as she tries the door and discovers it is unlocked, swinging slightly open.

2 CAPTION/Chace:
            At least the DOOR'S unlocked.

FOUR:
OTS PEACEKEEPER from panel Two, as CHACE gets into the car.

As she does, the cloak rides, up and exposes her BLOODIED PANT-LEG.

3 CAPTION/Chace:
            Old-fashion IGNITION, good...

FIVE:
POV PEACEKEEPER, CU of the BLOODIED PANT-LEG.

4 CAPTION/Chace:
            ...just need a few seconds...

SIX:
Angle in the car, as CHACE, wrapped in the black cloak, hotwires the ignition.

5 CAPTION/Chace:
            C'mon give a GIRL a BREAK...

SEVEN:
POV CHACE, looking in the rearview mirror, seeing the PEACEKEEPER approaching the vehicle, one hand out.

6 CAPTION/Chace: ...C'MON start...

EIGHT:
CU of the exhaust pipe, as a nice burst of black
exhaust comes out.

7 CAPTION/Chace: ...THANK YOU.

Page 20

ONE:
Angle as the CAR pulls away down the street,
leaving the PEACEKEEPER to wave his arms.

NO COPY.

TWO:
Another POV CHACE, checking the mirror, this one
on the side. PEACEKEEPER is visible getting on
his radio.

NO COPY.

THREE:
CHACE behind the wheel, pulling the cloak off
with her free hand as she drives. Looks pretty
determined.

NO COPY.

FOUR:
Angle on the CAR as it speeds along the broken
road out of Prizren. Passing some PEDESTRIANS as
they walk along the side of the road.

FIVE:
CHACE rolling down the window as she drives, now
out of the cloak.

NO COPY.

SIX:
Angle behind the car as CHACE sticks out an
arm, holding the cloak, which is snapping in the
wind.

NO COPY.

SEVEN:
The cloak, fluttering in the air as it falls, the
CAR already in the distance as she really floors
it.

NO COPY.

Page 21

ONE:
Large panel, bird's eye shot, as the CAR makes it's way along the narrow road. Broken countryside, still recovering from the war.

NO COPY.

TWO:
Another angle on the CAR as it passes an EXCAVATION at the side of the road, U.N. PEACEKEEPERS working backhoes, wearing surgical masks.

Basically, she's passing a mass grave, but we're being subtle about it.

The SUN is strong overhead.

NO COPY.

THREE:
Angle past the CAR as it slows. In BG, ahead of the vehicle, we can see the GERMAN SECTOR CHECKPOINT.

A SIGN on the side of the road, bent and bullet-marked, says:

PRISTINA 62 KM

[*And if we can get that in the proper language, even better, but I don't know what it would be...*] [22]

NO COPY.

22. This is the first instance of what would become a very real problem for me in the later story arcs; that of language. The comic book convention of using carets (</>) to denote speaking a foreign tongue seemed to me very coy and ill-suited to a spy story; especially when there would be times when not understanding what was being said would be as important and being able to follow it. In this instance, it's simply a detail for added verisimilitude; in later issues (especially around 13-15), it became much more important.

ONE:
OTS CHACE, behind the wheel. Through the windshield
we can see a GERMAN STAFFED CHECKPOINT. A GERMAN
FLAG is visible flying from the side of a tent.

1 CAPTION/Chace:
                    Now we LEARN if that bloke got the
                    LICENSE on this thing or NOT.

TWO:
Angle from seat, looking at CHACE as she smiles
brilliantly at the young SOLDIER who has stopped
her.

2 YOUNG SOLDIER:
                    <Where are you heading?>

3 CHACE: <Pristina.>

THREE:
From outside of the car, ANOTHER GUARD at the
checkpoint, reaching for a satellite phone. YOUNG
SOLDIER at CHACE'S WINDOW.

CHACE is handing him a billfold.

4 YOUNG SOLDIER:
                    <You have your PASS?>

5 CHACE: <Here.>

FOUR:
OTS YOUNG SOLDIER as he flips open the billfold and
removes a FOLDED PIECE OF PAPER.

NO COPY.

FIVE:
POV YOUNG SOLDIER as he unfolds the PAPER. A
WALLET-SIZE PHOTO has been folded in with it, and
falls free.

The PAPER, such as we can see, has the U.N. LOGO
on it.

6 YOUNG SOLDIER: <What's this?>

SIX:
OTS CHACE, a very slight smile, as the YOUNG
SOLDIER bends to pick up the photograph.

The OTHER SOLDIER is still on the satellite phone
in BG.

7 CHACE:
                    <Oh… uh, nothing, it's NOTHING…>

SEVEN:
CU SOLDIER, as he rises holding the PHOTOGRAPH,

the PAPER now forgotten in his other hand. His
eyes are wide with surprise and the beginning of
some amusement.

8 CHACE/off: <…can I just have that BACK?>

9 YOUNG SOLDIER:
                <One moment, please.>

Page 23

ONE:
Angle past CHACE as YOUNG SOLDIER approaches
the OTHER SOLDIER, beckoning him to get off the
phone.

1 CAPTION/Chace:
                That's right, that's it, ignore
                the PASS…

TWO:
POV CHACE, watching as YOUNG SOLDIER shows the
PHOTOGRAPH to OTHER SOLDIER, gesturing back at
Chace/us.

YOUNG SOLDIER appears amused. OTHER SOLDIER looks
vaguely bewildered.

2 CAPTION/Chace:
                …it's a FORGERY after ALL…

THREE:
Stet previous, but closer, and now YOUNG SOLDIER,
still holding the PHOTOGRAPH for OTHER SOLDIER,
is smiling at Chace/us. The OTHER SOLDIER is
grinning, very amused.

3 CAPTION/Chace:
                …and DON'T pay any ATTENTION to
                the BLOOD on my TROUSER LEG…

FOUR:
Stet previous, OTHER SOLDIER is still grinning
our way. YOUNG SOLDIER is smiling, coming back,
folding the paper with one hand, still holding the
PHOTOGRAPH.

4 CAPTION/Chace:
                …just look at the PICTURE, that's
                FINE.

FIVE:
Angle outside the car, past YOUNG SOLDIER as he
hands the PAPER back to CHACE.

CHACE looks embarrassed.

5 YOUNG SOLDIER:
                <Everything appears FINE. Have a

Sometimes Greg makes me draw nudie pictures!

SAFE trip.>

6 CHACE: <May I have, my...uh...>

7 YOUNG SOLDIER:
          <Yes, of course, sorry. The picture is of YOU?>

SIX:
          Reverse, from inside the car, and CHACE is taking the PHOTOGRAPH back from the YOUNG SOLDIER.
YOUNG SOLDIER looks almost sheepish. CHACE still looks embarrassed.

8 CHACE: <It's for my BOYFRIEND.>

10 YOUNG SOLDIER:
               <Of course, of course...>

SEVEN:
POV CHACE, putting the PHOTOGRAPH[23] back in the PAPER, and now, of course, we get to see it.

It's a picture of her, nude, posing on a bed. *Playboy* quality, <u>not</u> *Penthouse*![24]

11 YOUNG SOLDIER:
               <...drive CAREFULLY.>

12 CHACE: <Thank you.>

23. This is a complete and total steal from The Sandbaggers, though used here with a new wrinkle. In The Sandbaggers, one of the agents gets past a roadblock in Russia by "accidentally" handing over a stack of "novelty postcards." It seemed to me that, if the agent in question were female, and the picture was of herself, you might potentially get an even better reaction, since the instinctive response to another's embarrassment is to let them off the hook—and thus, send Tara on her way as quickly as possible.

24. As you can see from the collection of Steve's sketches, we spent a lot of time on this, and not for the prurient reasons, no matter what you may be thinking. The picture had to be the right one; innocent enough to be forgiven, but compromising enough to be adequately embarrassing. I think I sent Steve back on the sketches three or four times, and I'm sure, at the end, he thought I was just trying to get a stack of naked Tara's for some perverse purpose. All I can say to that is Steve's the one who held onto the sketches, not me.
   Very important moment, in my opinion.

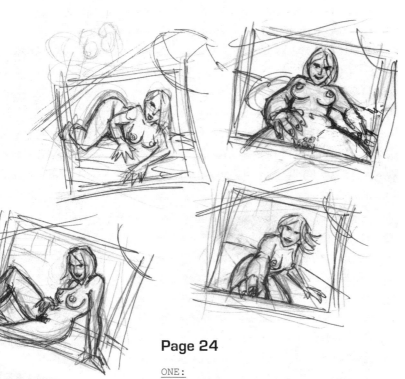

more "come hither" + amateurish

Page 24

<u>ONE:</u>
Exterior of the BRITISH H.Q., in PRISTINA.

The CAR is parked beside a couple of JEEPS, a TANK,
the appropriate Peacekeeping force vehicles.

BRITISH SOLDIERS mill about, doing their thing.

A HUT is to one side.

1 CHACE/hut: Sergeant Ramsey?…

<u>TWO:</u>
Interior of the hut, CHACE is standing in front of
a field-desk. RAMSEY, a staff sergeant in his late-
twenties, is rising and offering her a handshake.
She's accepting it. The hut is filled with maps and
papers and radio equipment.

2 CHACE: …my name's Chace, Tara Chace.

3 RAMSEY:

                I was getting WORRIED about you,
                Miss Chace. You were supposed to
                be here HOURS ago.

<u>THREE:</u>

CU CHACE, slight smile. She looks exhausted. Still in pain. But genuinely relieved to have made it this far.

4 CHACE: There was TRAFFIC on the ROAD.

FOUR:
Angle from the side, as RAMSEY sees CHACE'S wounded leg, reacting.

CHACE looking down, as if she'd forgotten about her injury.

5 RAMSEY: Good Lord, are you all right? You
                        want a MEDIC to take a look at
                        that?

6 CHACE: If it's not too much BOTHER.

FIVE:
Angle past CHACE, as she lowers herself into a chair. RAMSEY is passing her, heading out of the hut.

7 RAMSEY: Not at ALL. I'll be RIGHT BACK.

8 CHACE: Take your TIME…

SIX:
CU CHACE, now seated, eyes closing. Exhausted, safe. Smile.

9 CHACE: …take your time.

Page 25

ONE:
Interior of Crocker's Office, and it's about half the size of Weldon's, very Spartan. He's working at his desk, scribbling in a folder with a pen.

WALLACE is coming through the door. Past WALLACE, at the desk, we can see CROCKER'S PERSONAL ASSISTANT, KATE. Kate's in her mid-twenties, very pretty.

1 WALLACE: Boss?

2 CROCKER: What do you WANT, Tom?

TWO:
OTS CROCKER, looking up from his work, at WALLACE, who is leaning against the doorframe.

3 WALLACE: Signal from Istanbul Station.

4 WALLACE/linked:
                        Crow is on her way home.

THREE:
OTS WALLACE, CROCKER looking at him. No smile.
Considering. Seems vaguely satisfied with this
turn of events.

5 CROCKER: Is she all right?

6 WALLACE: She got CLIPPED in the leg, but it
               wasn't SERIOUS.

FOUR:
POV WALLACE, as CROCKER goes back to work.

7 CROCKER: Good.

8 CROCKER/linked:
               I'll want her REPORT on my DESK
               tomorrow.

FIVE:
WALLACE looking at CROCKER. Not quite incredulous.
CROCKER is ignoring him.

9 CROCKER: Was there something ELSE?

10 WALLACE: No, sir.

11 CROCKER: Then SHOVE OFF, Tom. I've got WORK
               to do.

SIX:
OTS CROCKER as WALLACE exits, shutting the door
behind him.

NO COPY.

SEVEN:
CROCKER, slight smile, putting pen back to
paper.

25. That no matter how much of a bastard Crocker is—to his superiors, his friends, his colleagues—we can see in this moment how much he honestly cares for his agents.

12 CROCKER/small: That's my girl.[25]

Queen & Country Issue Two

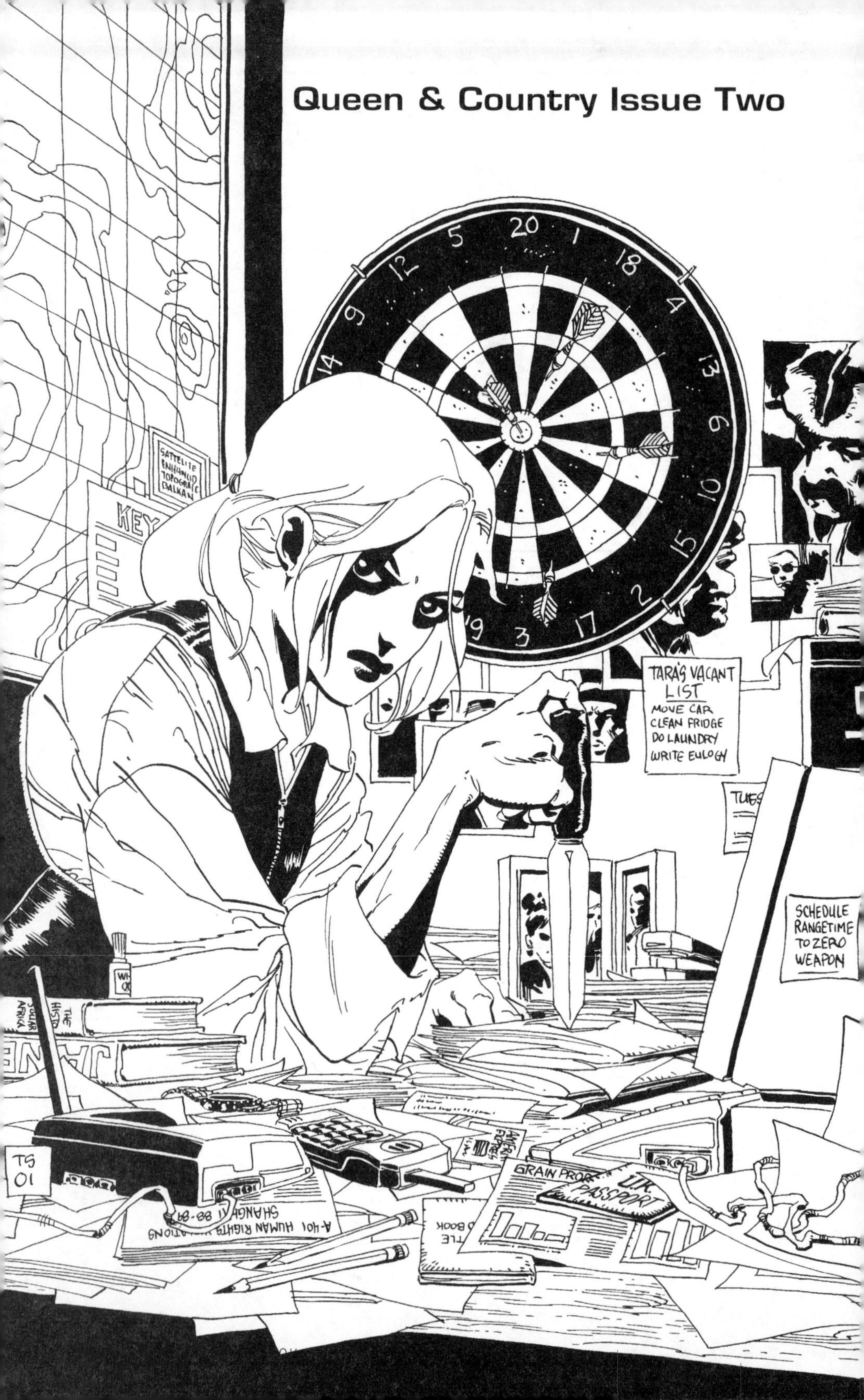
KEY
TARA'S VACANT LIST
MOVE CAR
CLEAN FRIDGE
DO LAUNDRY
WRITE EULOGY
SCHEDULE RANGETIME TO ZERO WEAPON
U.K. PASSPORT
TS 01

Page 1

ONE:
Establishing shot, London skyline—Big Ben, the Houses of Parliament, and, if possible, the MI6 Building across the Thames. [*Steve—there's actual reference for the building all over the Web and such, and there are some good shots of it at the start of the Bond film, The World is Not Enough*][1].

It is night, and it is raining rather heavily.

1 CAPTION: London.

TWO:
Angle on a lane on the top of a slight, bare, slope.[2] A VAN is parked to the side of the street, back to us.

Past the VAN, down the hillside and in the distance, we can see the MI6 Building in BG.

It's roughly three in the morning, and the streets are pretty darn bare. The rain is coming down hard enough to bounce off the street and VAN.

NO COPY.

THREE:
Angle as the driver's side door opens—remember we're in England—and a MAN steps out. The dome light in the van has been disabled, so there's not really any ambient light. MAN is perhaps in his mid-thirties, dressed like a casual laborer. Clean shaven. His pulling the hood up on his parka.

NO COPY.

FOUR:
Interior of the VAN, in the back, looking out as the MAN opens the DOORS. In FG, laying just inside the VAN, is a CRATE.

NO COPY.

FIVE:
Close angle, CU MAN'S HANDS, as he twists the

1 And no illustration can do this place justice. One of its nicknames is "Legoland." Seriously. Looks like some very obsessive-compulsive kids built this giant pyramid-esque structure along the Thames. "What's that wild looking building?" "Oh, that? That's the headquarters of British Secret Intelligence."
Truth is so much stranger than fiction.

2 Utter fiction. No such slope. This we call "dramatic license."

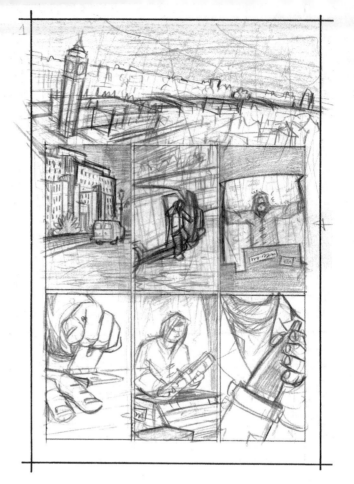

latches on the CRATE. We can see that he has TATTOOS on his FINGERS [*Steve—these are Russian Mob flags, and they each mean something different… I'll see if I can find a source for you*].[3]

The CRATE is labeled in CYRILLIC, with phrases such as CAUTION and EXPLOSIVE.

NO COPY.

SIX:
Close angle, from behind the open trunk, looking just over the lid as MAN lifts out a ROCKET LAUNCHER.[4]

NO COPY.

SEVEN:
Close angle, CU as MAN drops a ROCKET down the TUBE.

NO COPY.

3. I've found several references to this kind of tattooing in various places, but I've rarely encountered anything definitive. My understanding is that, for the most part, the tattoos act as credentials of a sort—symbol X means the subject is a stone-cold killer, etc.
In 2002, the Russian Interior Ministry estimated that somewhere between 70 to 80 percent of private businesses and banks in the country were paying out to some sort of protection or extortion racket of one form or another (MSNBC, August 31, 2002). In 1997, the Center for Strategice and International Studies (a non-partisan organization) estimated that Russian Organized Crime had 200 separate groups operating in some 58 countries around the world.

4. Not sure what the weapon system I was thinking of here. Not that it much matters—right now, there are so many shoulder-launched missile systems available on the black market around the world, it's giving intelligence agencies nightmares. Here, the rocket is being used to attack a building; it could just as easily have been directed at an aircraft. Note, I say just as easily; not just as successfully.

Pages 2 and 3

Lay this out in two tiers across each page. Upper tier is our interiors of MI6, lower tier is the rocket man. Perhaps if the panels of the upper tier slightly overlap the top of the panels in the lower tier we'll get the chronological, this-is-happening-at-the-same-time effect I'm after here.. Panels 1 through 6 are upper, 7 through 12 are lower.

ONE:
First tier.

Interior MI6 Building. This is a pretty drab and dull looking industrial corridor, with offices along both sides of the hall. In FG, A JANITOR, probably not white, is mopping the hallway. A PASS dangles from a chain around his neck.

TWO JUNIOR SIS OFFICERS are walking down the hallway, coming at us from BG. One of them carries a FILE of some sort. ALBERT is white, in his late twenties, wearing glasses. Looks like he's been up all night.

JILL is also white, female, also late twenties.

1 ALBERT:
                ...then shouting at the RUSSIAN
                desk.

2 JILL:
                And what did his EMINENCE D. Ops
                want?

TWO:
First tier.

Angle off ALBERT, as he opens an office door,
allowing JILL to enter. It's a small office, in
the Intelligence division, and there's a wall of
file cabinets, as well as a desk with a computer.
WINDOWS are behind the desk. The desk itself is
cluttered with papers.

3 ALBERT:
                Trying to track transfers from St.
                Petersburg to London Maritime Bank
                or some such.

4 ALBERT/linked:
                Though why this has CROCKER'S
                knickers in a TWIST I've no CLUE.

THREE:
First tier.

OTS ALBERT as he drops his FILE onto his desk.

JILL has stopped inside the doorway, now leaning
back against the wall, looking at ALBERT.

5 JILL:
                Well, he's planning a SPECIAL OP
                most like, isn't he?

6 ALBERT: Undoubtedly. Who knows? Maybe
                he'll even get PERMISSION first[5].

FOUR:
First tier.

OTS JILL, as ALBERT straightens up behind his
desk.

Behind ALBERT, through the window, we can only see
the London skyline, no hint of the rocket.

7 JILL:
                You mean the way he cleared Chace's
                run in Kosovo?

8 ALBERT:
                Could do. I hear they're
                forecasting SNOW in HELL later
                today, as well.

5.The second reference to Crocker's
habit of "shooting first, asking questions
later," in two issues.

FIVE:
First tier.

Angle as JILL turns to leave the office. ALBERT,
behind his desk, is frowning at the papers arrayed
before him.

9 ALBERT/small:
> We're going to be at this ALL
> night.

10 JILL:
> With that in mind, you want a
> coffee?

SIX:
First tier.

JILL holding in the doorway, as ALBERT looking up
to give her a grateful smile.

11 ALBERT:
> You'd be saving my LIFE, Jill—

SEVEN:
Second tier.

From the side of the VAN as the MAN steps back.

Past him we can see the MI-6 BUILDING, a gleaming
and somewhat inviting target. A couple lights on
in the building.

NO COPY.

EIGHT:
Second tier.

From behind the MAN as he hoists the LAUNCHER onto
his shoulder, sighting the building.

12 MAN/small:
> <Fuck with US...>

NINE:
Second tier.

ECU MAN'S hand on the grip, finger pulling the
trigger.

13 MAN:
> <...we fuck you BACK.>[6]

TEN:
Second tier.

From behind the MAN, a TRAIL of FLAME and SMOKE
from the launch blast, as the ROCKET speeds
towards the MI-6 BUILDING in BG.

NO COPY.

6. For the novel Critical Space, I had a
major character who was Russian, and
I wanted to pepper her speech with
appropriate words and phrases. I picked
up a couple of books, including one on
colloquial Russian...and discovered
that, apparently, profanity in Russian is
something glorious to behold. Insults
are graded into different tiers, and some
of them are incredibly inventive. This
has lead to my habit of giving Russian
characters very foul mouths, indeed,
most recently seen in Q&C 26-29, and
the Q&C novel, A Gentleman's Game.

ELEVEN:
Second tier.

Stet previous, but the ROCKET is receding rapidly, towards the building.

NO COPY.

TWELVE:
Second tier.

Stet previous, still behind the MAN, who is still holding the launcher on his shoulder.

There's no sign of the rocket, no trail, no light, no smoke. It's basically disappeared against the face of the building.

NO COPY.

Page 4

ONE:
Same angle as Twelve, previous, but MAN is now turning away from the building in BG, dropping the LAUNCHER off his shoulder.

In BG, we can see the EXPLOSION as the ROCKET detonates against the building. A flash of violent light, perhaps even some debris illuminated by the flame.[7]

NO COPY.

TWO:
Profile of the MAN, as he replaces the LAUNCHER in the back of the VAN. He's white, Russian, and thuggish, though only two of those facts are really going to be apparent. He's got a self-satisfied sneer going.

Rain drops drip from his hood and nose.

NO COPY.

THREE:
High angle, looking down at the VAN, as MAN gets behind the wheel once more.

NO COPY.

FOUR:
High angle, looking down, as we see the VAN driving away on the lane to one side of the panel as EMERGENCY VEHICLES come streaming in on a separate road, heading for the SMOKING MI6 BUILDING.

NO COPY.

7. On Wednesday, 20 September, 2000, the SIS building was attacked in similar manner. The weapon used was a Russian-built MK 22 anti-tank rocket—a very small and compact weapon system, so I've been given to believe. The attack was believed to have been carried out by the Real IRA, an IRA splinter group. The attack hit the eighth floor of the building, though SIS was, as you might expect, circumspect about the damage the blast caused. I've done occasional looking since this incident, and have utterly failed to find any more information about who was responsible, or whether or not the attacker(s) were apprehended.

Page 5

ONE:
Small   establishing   shot,   exterior,   South
Kensington[8], same night, still raining. We're
looking at a row of townhouses.

The street is empty, cars parked all along.

TWO:
Interior of CHACE'S BEDROOM. We're looking down on
her from an angle above and beyond the foot of her
bed, so we can take in the whole room.

The room is something of a mess. Clothes and papers
are strewn about. A couple empty liquor bottles
are scattered on the floor. The nightstand has a
LAMP, CLOCK, PHONE, PAGER, and ANOTHER BOTTLE of
scotch, half-empty.

CHACE herself is asleep on the bed, sprawled out
in a torment of bedclothes. She's sleeping in
a t-shirt and underwear, and while she's mostly
covered, her wounded leg is free of the sheets,
and we can see the BANDAGE on her leg.

1 SFX: brrt brrt

THREE:
Angle from the nightstand, looking past the CLOCK,
PHONE, and BOTTLE, at CHACE, now painfully awake,
pulling the phone to her ear.

The CLOCK reads 3:57 A.M..

2 SFX: brrt br—

3 CHACE:
                Chace.

FOUR:
Angle, CHACE on her back, hand over her eyes, as
she puts the RECEIVER to her ear.

4 TAILLESS/elec:
                Duty Ops Officer. From D. Ops,
                MINDERS to the Ops Room.

5 CHACE:
                Ten minutes.

FIVE:
Stet previous, CHACE on her back. She's dropped
the RECEIVER beside her head, and uncovered her
eyes.

She looks exhausted, and mildly alarmed.

6 CHACE/small:
                Oh damn.

8. I chose this location for Chace's first flat—she's since moved in the series to Camden—for the simple reason that, when I first visited London as a wide-eyed innocent of 12 years old, traveling with my father, we stayed at a B & B in South Kensington, and I had a vague recollection of what some of the streets around there looked like.

SIX:
Angle from the nightstand side of the bed. In BG we can see the open door to the bathroom, the toilet visible, and perhaps the sink.

CHACE is tumbling out of the bed, lurching for the bathroom door.

7 CHACE: Oh damn...

SEVEN:
From the bedroom, looking into the bathroom, where CHACE is kneeling at the toilet, throwing up in BG.[9]

NO COPY.

9. Something you never see in James Bond, tell you that much.

Page 6

ONE:
Exterior of the MI6 BUILDING, still dark, still raining, but now there are TWO FIRE ENGINES parked outside the building, and EMERGENCY PERSONNEL are running back and forth.

CONSTABLES are on the scene, in their slickers, trying to control the area.

Angle up from street level, and we can see the blast damage, roughly five stories above. The ground is scattered with broken glass and chunks of the building.

NO COPY.

TWO:
Angle on the street, and we see a CONSTABLE leaning in at the driver's window of a just-parked car.

Emergency work continuing in BG.

1 CONSTABLE:
                    Move the vehicle, please...

THREE:
OTS CONSTABLE, as he steps back from the opening door.

CHACE is getting out, extending her pass towards the CONSTABLE'S FACE with one hand. She's not looking at him; rather, she's looking at the building.

She looks better, her hair pulled back. Wearing a shirt and jeans and jacket.

2 CONSTABLE:
                    ...you can't park here.

3 CHACE:
                    Yes, I can.

FOUR:
CU CHACE, her reaction to the damaged building.
She looks shocked.

4 CHACE/small:
                    Jesus.

FIVE:
Angle past the CONSTABLE, back to us in FG, as
CHACE, in BG, enters the building. CHACE is again
presenting her pass to the WARDEN on duty at the
door. The WARDEN is middle-aged, in an overcoat.

NO COPY.

Page 7

ONE:
Interior of the building, CHACE is being let
through a set of doors by another WARDEN. In BG,
we can see the first WARDEN at the front door, and,
jogging past him to catch CHACE, is WALLACE. CHACE
is turning her head in response to his call.

1 WALLACE: Tara!

TWO:
Through the second set of doors, CHACE is through
and waiting for WALLACE, who is addressing her as
he shows his pass to the WARDEN there.

2 WALLACE: What the hell happened?

3 CHACE: You're Head of Section, YOU tell
                ME.

THREE:
From the end of a hallway, CHACE and WALLACE
coming towards us. WARDEN in the EBG.

4 CHACE: I'm supposed to still be on
                DISABILITY.

5 WALLACE: There is no disability when Crocker
                SCRAMBLES the section.

FOUR:
Behind CHACE and WALLACE as they wait for the
elevator.

6 WALLACE: How ARE you feeling?

7 CHACE: Leg's fine, Tom.

FIVE:
Inside the elevator, CHACE leading, looking down

slightly. WALLACE is entering behind her, looking at her with some care.

8 WALLACE:

> They're both FINE, you ask me, but that's NOT what I meant.

9 CHACE:

> I know what you MEANT[10].

SIX:
In the elevator, WALLACE at one side, looking at CHACE. CHACE at the other, not returning the gaze.

NO COPY.

SEVEN:
Exterior of the elevator, doors open, CHACE coming forward. WALLACE still in the car.

NO COPY.

Page 8

ONE:
Interior of the Operations Room, and it's buzzing with activity. RON and ALEXIS are each on their posts, and there are THREE ADDITIONAL RUNNERS moving back and forth through the space, carrying papers or talking on telephones.

Behind RON'S POST, on the raised dais, are a couple of chairs. CROCKER is standing in the midst of them, smoking, and looking pretty damn pissed off. He's in the same three-piece suit he wore last time we saw him, though if you want to get tricky, maybe the tie is different.

In one of the chairs is the third member of the Special Section, EDWARD KITTERING. KITTERING is white, with unruly hair that's bordering on being just a little too long. He's wearing jeans and a sweatshirt. He's the youngest member of the Special Section, perhaps 24.

WALLACE and CHACE have just entered.

1 TAILLESS:

> ...rotating the surveillance...

2 TAILLESS:

> ...the M.O.D.[11] about short-range rockets...

3 TAILLESS:

> ...at the Home Office, sending someone from FIVE[12]...

10. A note on the use of caps, here. At this point in my ever-evolving script style, I used CAPS to indicate words I wanted emphasized. I stink at emphasis; I don't know why it is, because I believe I have a good ear for dialogue. But try as I might, I can't seem to place the emphasis in the right place most of the time. These days, I use bold to indicate emphasis, rather than caps—something that came about as a result for writing for Marvel during the Jemas-Quesada days, when they decided that dialogue needed to be in both upper and lower-case. My understanding is that someone somewhere at Marvel read something by someone that argued it was easier for kids to read if the words were in both upper and lower case. I personally think this is utter bullshit, but it was the editorial directive, and thus, my writing changed to reflect that. These days, I still use bold, because old habits die hard.

11. The Ministry of Defense.

12. Another example of how things change; if I knew then what I know now, the line would have read, "...sending someone from BOX..." as I have since learned that nobody refers to the Security Services as "Five" except for wannabes and authors of espionage comics.

4 CROCKER:

>Where the HELL have you two BEEN?

TWO:
OTS CROCKER, as WALLACE mounts the dais reaching for a chair. KITTERING is raising a hand in greeting.

CHACE is following.

5 WALLACE:

>The HONEYMOON was short but SWEET.

6 WALLACE/linked:

>Morning, Ed.

7 KITTERING:

>Hey, Tom.

8 KITTERING/linked:

>Tara. How's your leg?

THREE:
From behind KITTERING, WALLACE now seated, as CHACE takes the remaining chair. CROCKER stands over them, positively glowering.

9 CHACE:

>It works.

10 CHACE/linked:

>Sir.

11 CROCKER:

>Sit down, Tara.

Page 9

ONE:
Angle past RON at his desk, on his headset, rapidly shuffling through papers. A RUNNER is handing him a FOLDER.

In BG, we can see CROCKER standing, talking to CHACE, WALLACE, and KITTERING.

1 CROCKER:

>At SIX minutes before FOUR this morning, the FIFTH FLOOR was hit by a ROCKET ATTACK.

2 CROCKER/linked:

>Right now we don't know WHO, WHAT, or WHY.

TWO:
Angle behind WALLACE, with KITTERING partially in panel on the left, CHACE on the right. CROCKER is

this section has good examples of me figuring out how to fit lots of characters into each panel and still make the dialogue + composition flow decently.

TWLK

C WT KW

addressing the three of them. WALLACE is pulling a cigarette from his pack with his teeth.

3 CROCKER:
Intel is on with the M.O.D., trying to determine the nature of the weapon, and the POLICE have started a canvass.

THREE:
Kind of a three-shot, chair level, with KITTERING closest to us, then WALLACE, then CHACE.

CROCKER stands just inside the panel, and we can perhaps see his trousers, or his hand as he flicks ash.

KITTERING is leaning back. WALLACE is offering CHACE a cigarette from his pack, and she's taking it, speaking to CROCKER. All look very attentive and concerned.

4 CHACE:
How bad was it?

5 CROCKER:
Two dead, one wounded.

6 WALLACE:
We got off LIGHT.

FOUR:
CROCKER scowling. Past him, we can see WALLACE and CHACE passing a lighter between them.

KWCT

←CTWK

WK

7 CROCKER:
> That's NOT our problem.

8 CROCKER/linked:
> Our problem is we've been ATTACKED in our HOME, and that CANNOT stand.

FIVE:
KITTERING waving a gust of smoke away with one hand. CROCKER still glowering. Past KITTERING, we can see WALLACE, agreeing.

9 KITTERING:
> Not much we can do about that.

10 WALLACE:
> He's right, Boss. It's DOMESTIC.

Page 10

ONE:
CROCKER, not scowling so much as grimly adamant.

1 CROCKER:
> I don't CARE.

TWO:
CHACE, looking sideways at the Ops Room, as CROCKER and WALLACE argue.

2 WALLACE:
> We're not CHARTERED for domestic work, Boss, you know that. It's the PURVIEW of MI5.

3 CROCKER:

>Five wasn't ATTACKED, Tom. WE were.

THREE:
OTS CROCKER, WALLACE still arguing with him.

KITTERING and CHACE are exchanging glances.

4 CROCKER:

>The FOREIGN OFFICE will give us backing.

5 WALLACE:

>And the HOME OFFICE[13] will OPPOSE.

6 WALLACE/linked:

>I can SEE where you're HEADING, Boss…

FOUR:
Angle on RON, answering a PHONE. CROCKER, WALLACE, KITTERING, and CHACE as before in BG, but CROCKER and WALLACE are on the verge of each pissing the other seriously off.

7 WALLACE:

>…but if SIS goes mucking about in a FIVE investigation—

8 CROCKER:

>They can INVESTIGATE to their HEART'S CONTENT, Tom!

9 CROCKER/linked:

>That's NOT what I want!

FIVE:
Angle on CHACE, looking at the cigarette burning between her fingers. Eyes are kind of distant.

10 CHACE:

>What do you want, sir?

SIX:
CROCKER, calm, and perhaps dangerously serious.

11 CROCKER:

>Retaliation.

SEVEN:
CROCKER standing in front of CHACE, WALLACE, and KITTERING, all of them silent.

In BG, we can see still RON on the phone.

NO COPY.

13. Traditionally, the Foreign and Commonwealth Office has purview over SIS, since SIS technically operates only on foreign soil; the Security Services fall under the domain of the Home Office. Things get confused and rather tricky when talking about dominion, however; the Home Office tends to view those colonies/former colonies as their own territories.

Page 11

ONE:
Past RON, RECEIVER to his chest, turning to CROCKER, behind him. CROCKER turning to acknowledge RON.

WALLACE, CHACE, and KITTERING are still, silent. WALLACE is exhaling smoke.

1 RON:
> Sir? The Deputy Chief wants you in C's office.

2 CROCKER:
> Tell them I'm coming up.

TWO:
CROCKER turning back to address the three.

3 CROCKER:
> I want you three in the PIT, wait there 'til I NEED you…

THREE:
CU CROCKER using the toe of his shoe to kill his cigarette.

4 CROCKER/above:
> …I'll call when I'm done with C and Weldon.

FOUR:
OTS CROCKER as he starts to turn, WALLACE looking kinda pissy at him.

5 WALLACE:
> And while we WAIT, what? SHARPEN our KNIVES?

FIVE:
CROCKER snarling, heading for the door, without looking back. CHACE, WALLACE, and KITTERING watching his departure.

6 CROCKER:
> You can get digging, Tom.

7 CROCKER/linked:
> And ANOTHER crack like THAT, I'll find myself a NEW head of section.

SIX:
From behind KITTERING, CHACE, and WALLACE, as CROCKER exits in BG.

NO COPY.

SEVEN:
CHACE looking at WALLACE, slight eyebrow arch.

WALLACE looks pissed.

8 CHACE:

    Does that mean I get YOUR job?[14]

9 WALLACE:

    Sod off,[15] Tara.

14. We call this "foreshadowing," though it took us some 25 issues to execute it. What can I say, I like to take my time.

15. An example of a line I really wish I hadn't used. It reads as "forced British" to me, now.

Page 12

ONE:
Interior of C's Office. This is the nicest office in the building, obviously, and unlike Weldon's and Crocker's, it's got class. Large space, broken into two sections—one is the work area, marked by bookshelves, a desk with a computer, various appropriate desk items.

The other section is almost a small sitting room, with two small leather couches and a leather armchair, with a small coffee table and a couple end-tables. A tea and coffee service has been laid out on a tray on the table.

Wide establishing, from the sitting room portion, WELDON seated on one of the couches, back to us, with C seated in the easy chair.

C is in his late sixties, face clean shaven but lined, bushy eyebrow, dark and tiny eyes. He wears a hastily put on and ill-fitting suit. Looks like a wacky little old man, kind of.

1 WELDON:

    …should be here in half an hour.

2 C:

    He'll meet with Crocker.

TWO:
Angle past the coffee table, as C leans forward, using a POT to fill his CUP.

3 WELDON/off:

    I'm not certain that's WISE, sir—

4 C:

    Whatever HISTORY exists between them, they'll be PROFESSIONAL.

THREE:
Angle past WELDON, frowning. C is sitting back in his chair with his cup and saucer.

In BG, we can see the door to the office has opened and CROCKER is entering.

5 WELDON:

    Professional isn't the WORD I use to describe—

6 CROCKER:
> Sorry to keep you WAITING.

FOUR:
New angle, WELDON on the couch to the left,
C in his chair to the right, as CROCKER steps
forward.

7 C:
> You were in the Ops Room?

8 CROCKER:
> Yes, sir.

9 C:
> Anything?

FIVE:
OTS C as CROCKER, still standing, bends to fix
himself a cup of coffee.

10 CROCKER:
> We're still waiting to hear from
> the M.O.D. about the
weapon.
11 CROCKER:
> Hopefully that will give us a
> LEAD.

SIX:
OTS CROCKER, straightening. WELDON on the couch—
and it's important here to note that while WELDON
and CROCKER don't often agree and can often barely
stand one another, they really are professionals,
so when Weldon disagrees, he's not just being
contrary—leaning slightly forward.

C is now looking at WELDON.

12 WELDON:
> Unlikely, don't you think, Paul?
13 WELDON/linked:
> These days one can buy a ROCKET
> LAUNCHER at any corner STORE.

14 CROCKER:
> I am AWARE, sir…

Page 13

ONE:
Side angle, CROCKER turning to address the rest
to C, who appears engrossed in the contents of
his cup.

1 CROCKER:
> …but right now that's all we
> have.

2 C:
> You'll give whatever you LEARN to
> FIVE, of course.

TWO:
CROCKER still standing, C now looking up, as
WELDON growls.

3 CROCKER:
> I'll SHARE it with them, yes sir.

4 WELDON:
> It's an ACADEMIC distinction.

5 CROCKER:
> I don't think it is.

THREE:
OTS CROCKER, C again musing at his cup, WELDON
getting testy.

6 WELDON:
> It'll be THEIR investigation.

7 CROCKER:
> It was OUR people who were MURDERED.
> I'm not about to let those PRATS in
> FIVE speak for them.

FOUR:
OTS C, as WELDON and CROCKER stare at one
another.

NO COPY.

FIVE:
Reverse, now looking at C in his chair, CROCKER
and WELDON on each side, as before.

8 C:
> Those PRATS, as you put it,
> Paul, are our COLLEAGUES in
> INTELLIGENCE.

9 C/linked:
> Implying that departmental RIVALRY
> will influence the QUALITY of their
> investigation is CHILDISH.

SIX:
OTS C, looking at CROCKER, who looks somewhat
chastised.

10 C:
> Don't you think?

11 CROCKER:
> It's not the QUALITY I'm worried
> about, sir, but the RESULT.

SEVEN:
WELDON, settling back in his seat, somewhat
mollified.

12 WELDON:
>   They'll see the responsible parties
>   IDENTIFIED and IMPRISONED.

13 CROCKER/off:
>   I don't WANT them imprisoned...

EIGHT:
OTS CROCKER, C and WELDON'S reactions. C is mildly
aback at Crocker's statement, but WELDON looks
like he might burst a vessel.

14 CROCKER:
>   ...I want them DEAD.

Page 14

ONE:
Interior of The Pit, which is slang for the
Special Operations Officer's offices. [How's that
for a confusing sentence?]

This is a room with THREE DESKS arrayed around the
space, one facing away from each wall, with the
exception of the entry wall, which is bare but for
a couple of filing cabinets.

Nearest the door is WALLACE'S DESK, which is a
pretty clean, with TWO PHONES—one red—some files,
and a PC.

CHACE'S DESK is opposite the door, and is a mess,
covered with papers which have pretty much buried
the computer.

KITTERING'S DESK is opposite Wallace's, and is a
mixture of the two.

A MAP OF THE WORLD is on one wall, and a DART BOARD
is positioned on the wall above CHACE'S DESK.

Only other detail of importance is that by the
door, perhaps on the filing cabinets, are THREE
DUFFEL BAGS, each of them different from one
another. These are the agent's go-bags, the ones
they grab when they have to hustle.

WALLACE is throwing darts at the BOARD while CHACE
leans back in her chair, legs up on the desk,
apparently unconcerned with the sharp pointed
objects flying about two feet over her head. A
couple DARTS are already imbedded in the BOARD.

KITTERING is seated, and actually looks like he's
working.

1 WALLACE:

>   Sure you don't want to run to the
>   COMMISSARY and grab yourself an
>   APPLE?

2 WALLACE/linked:

>   I do a MEAN William Tell.

3 CHACE:

>   You're a RIOT, Tom.

4 CHACE/linked:

>   He's a riot, isn't he?

5 KITTERING:

>   If you mean the kind with PROPERTY
>   DAMAGE and LOSS of LIFE, then
>   yes.[16]

16. This was Jamie S. Rich's favorite line this issue. For a while, every time I'd turn in a script, he'd either call or email me with his notes, and then deliver a verdict on "favorite line." In issue 1, it was the bit about the bullets marked "to whom it may concern."

TWO:
Past KITTERING, looking up at WALLACE. WALLACE,
last dart in hand, ready to throw, is glancing at
KITTERING.

CHACE looking at WALLACE, amused.

6 WALLACE:

>   I'll remember you said that when
>   I'm preparing your ANNUAL review.

7 KITTERING:

>   You don't SCARE me…

THREE:
From the DART BOARD as WALLACE'S throw nails the
BULL'S EYE. Below, CHACE is looking at KITTERING,
grinning.

8 KITTERING:

>   …she'll have YOUR job by the end of
>   the DAY.

9 KITTERING:

>   You'll be NICE to me, won't you
>   Tara?

10 CHACE:

>   Do you SWEAR ever-lasting LOYALTY,
>   to live and die at my COMMAND?

FOUR:
OTS CHACE, KITTERING holding up his hands in mild
protest.

10 KITTERING:

>   I fear I have CONFUSED you with
>   someone ELSE.

11 KITTERING/linked:

>   I thought you were Tara Chace, NOT
>   Paul Crocker.

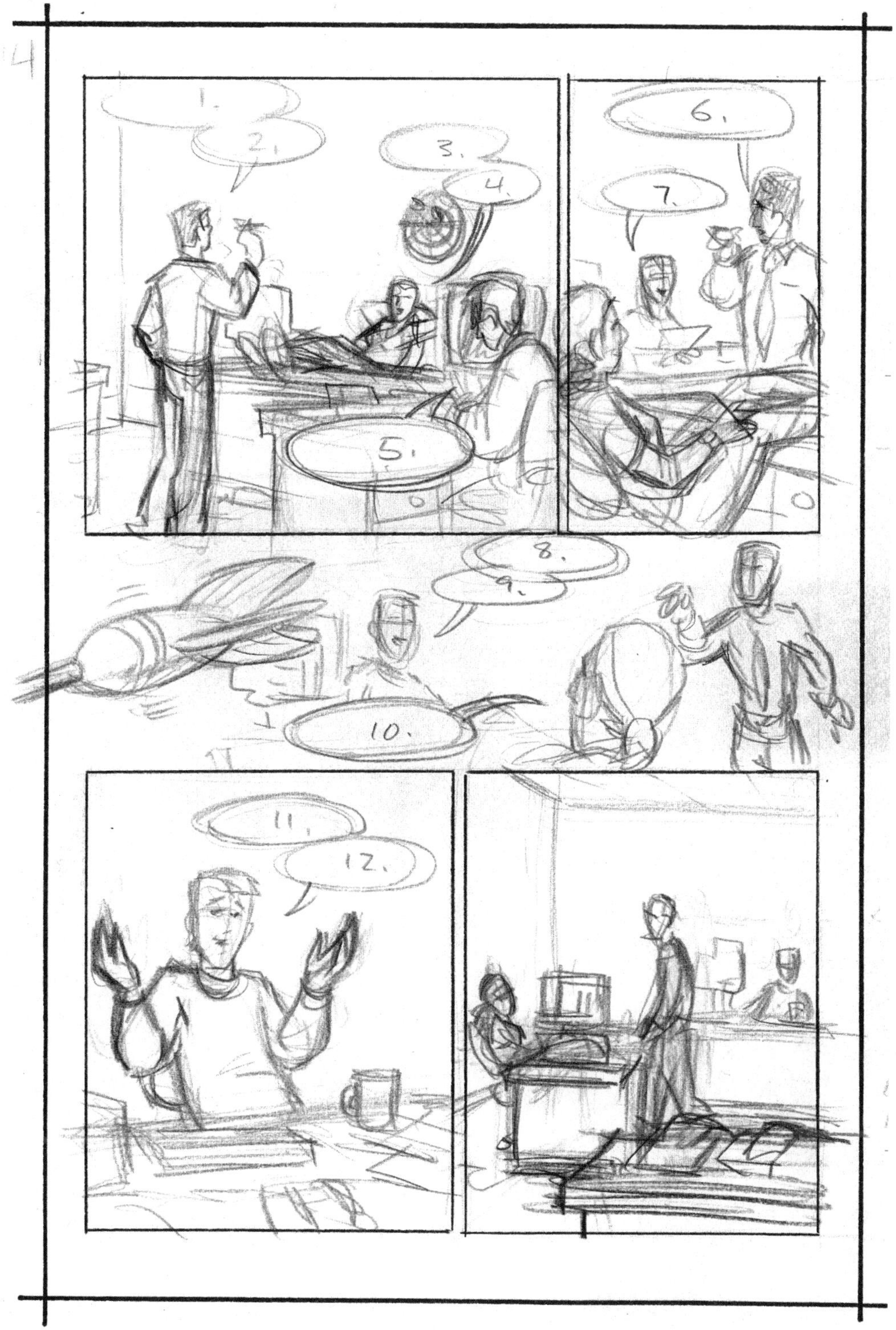
4
1.
2.
3.
4.
5.
6.
7.
8.
9.
10.
11.
12.

FIVE:
FIVE:
Wide, the THREE AGENTS, momentarily silent, in
thought.

NO COPY.

Page 15

ONE:
Angle past WALLACE, as he pulls the DARTS from the
board. CHACE, beneath him, looking up to address
him.

1 CHACE:
          Rocket hit the Fifth Floor?

2 WALLACE:
          Yes.

3 CHACE:
          Who was working up there?

TWO:
Past KITTERING, as WALLACE turns to head back to
his throwing position. CHACE'S attention still on
WALLACE.

4 KITTERING:
          Jill Baron, Albert Cooper, and
          a fellow from MAINTENANCE named
          Ravi.

5 CHACE:
          Baron and Cooper were on the
          Russian Desk.

6 WALLACE:
          It's COINCIDENCE…

THREE:
OTS CHACE, as WALLACE turns, preparing to throw
again.

7 WALLACE:
          …they weren't the TARGET.

8 CHACE:
          Not SPECIFICALLY, no…

FOUR:
CU CHACE, thinking. Gosh, she's purty.[17]

9 CHACE/below:
          …we were.

FIVE:
Past CHACE, looking at KITTERING, who now has his
chin resting in his hand. WALLACE appears deeply

engrossed in his dart game.

10 KITTERING:

     You mean ALL of us, the SERVICE.

11 CHACE:

     Very deft, Ed. You should be a SPY.

12 KITTERING:

     Is the Boss SERIOUS? About RETALIATION and all that?

SIX:
WALLACE and CHACE exchanging looks. WALLACE is poised for another throw.

NO COPY.

SEVEN:
ECU of the DART burying itself into the BOARD, dead on.[18]

NO COPY.

17. I'm often at odds with myself about Chace's appearance, her looks. I have always imagined her as attractive, certainly sexy, and often beautiful...but of that kind of beauty that ebbs and flows, depending on situation and circumstance. To my mind, she's never more attractive than when she's being smart, when she's doing her job, and doing it well. For that reason, every so often in a script I'll have a note like this, where I feel almost embarrassed about pointing out the fact.

18. Note the rather terse description of this panel, and then compare it to what Steve did, and how Steve constructed the whole page to lead to this panel. This is why Steve Rolston kicks ass.

ONE:
Interior of C's Office, and CROCKER and WELDON are arguing. C is rising from his chair.

1 WELDON:
…turn EVERYTHING into your own PERSONAL crusade?[19]

2 CROCKER:
It's not MY crusade, it's for the good of the Service!

TWO:
C, who is rather small, comparatively, is heading for his desk, as CROCKER and WELDON continue.

3 CROCKER:
If we're not seen to take EVERY measure to PROTECT and AVENGE our people, how can we expect them to TRUST us![20]

4 WELDON:
There is a LITTLE thing called PATRIOTISM, Paul, perhaps you've HEARD of it?

THREE:
View across C's DESK, as C takes a PIPE from a small rack with one hand, opening a TIN of TOBACCO with the other.

In BG, CROCKER is railing at WELDON. WELDON is on his feet, giving as good as he gets.

5 CROCKER:
Patriotism doesn't GUARANTEE loyalty, it only INITIATES it!

6 WELDON:
And the UNSPOKEN corollary to your code of VENGEANCE is what, exactly?

7 WELDON/linked:
Betray us at the COST of your LIFE?

FOUR:
OTS WELDON, on CROCKER, and he's deadly serious.

8 CROCKER:
If it prevents another PHILBY or MACLEAN or BURGESS, yes, sir.[21]

FIVE:
CU on C, who is lighting his pipe. An eyebrow is arching. He's listening, all right.

19. This is another mistake, and a minor one, I admit, but worth pointing out for those of you who are interested in the choices I make. I started this line with an ellipsis—"…"—but I should have started it with an em-dash—"—"—to indicate that we were joining the scene late, and that the dialogue had already been flying.

20. This establishes another recurring theme for the series, and one that plays a huge part in the first Q&C novel, A Gentleman's Game.

21. The so-called "Cambridge Spies." Guy Burgess, Donald MacLean, and Kim Philby all served as double-agents within the British Government, working for the Soviets. There's been much speculation as to how they were able to penetrate so successfully and so deeply without rousing suspicion, something that, in turn, has been attributed to the "old-boys network"—the idea that these men were Englishmen, dammit, who had come from the "best schools" and were therefore beyond reproach or suspicion! Philby, in particular, has held a particular fascination for spy writers and espionage aficionados; John LeCarre's fabulous Tinker, Tailor, Soldier, Spy, is just one of many works inspired by this betrayal.
Peter Wright's Spycatcher—which was banned in the UK for violating the Official Secrets Act—was one of the first books to speculate that the Cambridge Three were actually Four…or potentially even more.
Theories continue to this day, some of them going so far as to suggest, or even outright declare, that the Security Services, and even SIS, had moles working at the highest levels.
Crocker's vehemence here was meant to illustrate two things—first, his absolute commitment to his job; second, his absolute commitment to his people (something the series touches on again and again in later stories).

In BG, WELDON is still facing CROCKER, calmer now. CROCKER is just as defiant and arrogant.

9 WELDON:

> I see.

SIX:
ECU C'S hand, as he puts the extinguished MATCH into his ashtray.

10 WELDON/off:

> And if the WHOLE of S.I.S. serves in FEAR, that's just a HAPPY by-product?

SEVEN:
Angle on C, puffing on his pipe, raising his right hand to indicate that he wants the argument to stop. WELDON and CROCKER in BG. C's not looking at them at all, but rather past us.

11 CROCKER:

> Of course not! But RELYING on the OLD BOY—

12 C:

> That's ENOUGH.

EIGHT:
Angle past CROCKER and WELDON, looking at C'S back. C has lowered his hand.

Past C, we can see, through the window, that dawn is breaking.

13 C:

> Why don't you leave us ALONE, Donald?

NINE:
Angle from C'S door as WELDON exits, scowling. In BG, CROCKER is approaching C's DESK, while C continues to look out the window.

NO COPY.

Page 17

ONE:
Looking at C, puffing on his pipe, looking out the window. CROCKER just at his shoulder, frowning, looking out the window, as well.

1 C:

> Donald Weldon is the Deputy Chief.

2 C/linked:

> He demands—rightly—the RESPECT due him.

TWO:
Stet previous, but C has turned to look up at
CROCKER. CROCKER is frowning and now looking down,
not wanting to meet his gaze.

3 CROCKER:
                    I do RESPECT him.

4 C:
                    You respect the POSITION, not the
                    MAN. An ATTITUDE that will get
                    your into TROUBLE, Paul.

THREE:
Angle past CROCKER, still standing as before, as
C takes his seat behind the desk.

5 C:
                    You're   MARGINALLY   easier   to
                    REPLACE than he is.

6 C/linked:
                    Don't FORCE me to CHOOSE.

FOUR:
Past C, now seated, adjusting his pipe, as CROCKER
continues looking out the window, no longer
frowning, but now just looking like a chastised
teenager.

7 CROCKER:
                    Understood, sir.

8 C:
                    It so happens that I agree with
                    you. An ATTACK like this MUST be
                    answered. And we must be SEEN to
                    answer it.

FIVE:
OTS CROCKER, looking at C, now, who is gazing
up at him. C holds the PIPE in position with one
hand.

9 CROCKER:
                    Then let me use the MINDERS to—

10 C:
                    Answering   it   does   not   mean
                    MURDER.

SIX:
C opening one of the files on his desk, dismissing
CROCKER.

11 C:
                    David Kinney will be in your office
                    in ten minutes.

12 C/linked:
                    I expect you to COOPERATE with
                    him.

SEVEN:
CROCKER looking at C, who is now pretty much
ignoring him.

NO COPY.

EIGHT:
From the door, as CROCKER opens it. He's cranky,
but trying to hide it.

C is working at his desk in BG.

13 C:
                I mean it, Paul.

14 CROCKER:
                Yes, sir.

Page 18

ONE:
ANTE-ROOM TO CROCKER'S OFFICE, as he blows through
the door. KATE, working at her desk, is looking
up.

1 CROCKER:
                Kate, call the U.S. Embassy, find
                out if Franks[22] is free for lunch.

2 KATE:
                Can I tell him what it's about?

3 CROCKER:
                He'll KNOW.

TWO:
Interior CROCKER'S OFFICE, as CROCKER continues
in, jamming a cigarette into his mouth.

KATE, at her desk in the ante-room, is rising,
looking after him.

4 KATE:
                David Kinney is being ESCORTED up
                from RECEPTION.

5 CROCKER:
                Any chance he'll get LOST on the
                WAY?

6 KATE:
                The Wardens are OLD, but not THAT
                old.

THREE:
CROCKER falling into his chair, lighting his
cigarette, as KATE steps out again, shutting the
door after her.

22. Franks? Who the hell is "Franks?" I hear you cry.

I do this a lot, too. I change names. I change names two or three times during the course of a story, sometimes, and I don't always manage to catch them all before I send out the script/story/ whatever. For those of you who know the series, this line should read, "Cheng," and the pronouns that follow should all be feminine, rather than masculine. At this time, though, I had thought that the CIA Station Chief in London would be a man named, yes, Franks. No idea what his first name was going to be. Not even sure why I ultimately changed it, but I suspect it was because I didn't want Tara to be the only woman in a position of authority—all the other female characters presented thus far (here Kate, Crocker's Personal Assistant, and earlier Alexis, the Main Communications Officer) had been in subordinate staff positions, and it mattered to me that there be at least one other female character in a position of power.

7 CROCKER:
>Send him in when he gets here.

8 KATE:
>Yes, sir.

FOUR:
Angle from corner, CROCKER glaring at the closed door.

NO COPY.

FIVE:
Past the ASHTRAY on the DESK, CROCKER has turned his chair and is staring at a wall, deep in thought, cigarette dangling from his lower lip.

NO COPY.

SIX:
From the back of the office, above CROCKER, as the DOOR OPENS, and KATE leans in.

9 KATE:
>David Kinney, sir.

10 CROCKER:
>Thanks, Kate.

Page 19

ONE:
Two-shot, as CROCKER rises and offers a hand to KINNEY. Kinney is, essentially, Crocker's opposite number at MI5, which is part of the reason they hate one another. KINNEY is Crocker's age, stockier, mustached, in a suit.

They're both acting like they're pleased to see each other.

1 CROCKER:
>David.

2 KINNEY:
>Paul.

3 CROCKER:
>Take a PEW.

TWO:
OTS CROCKER, still on his feet, as KINNEY sits in one of the chairs in front of the desk.

4 KINNEY:
>Bad business. Sorry about YOUR people.

5 CROCKER:
>Yes. Thanks.

6 CROCKER/linked:
>What have you got?

THREE:
KINNEY, seated, smoothing his tie.

7 KINNEY:
>We're less than SIX HOURS into our investigation.

8 KINNEY/linked:
>What makes you think we have ANYTHING?

FOUR:
OTS KINNEY, as CROCKER, who has come around to front of the desk, leans back, arms folded. Cigarette still burns between fingers.

9 CROCKER:
>The fact that you'd sooner eat BROKEN GLASS than ask for my HELP.

FIVE:
Reverse, OTS CROCKER as he takes a drag on his smoke. KINNEY grinning. Barely friendly.

10 KINNEY:
>And the fact that YOU'D rather FELLATE a PONY than give it to ME.[23]

23. This was the "second favorite line" of the issue.

SIX:
POV CROCKER, on KINNEY, who is now seriously smiling in a very smug way.

11 KINNEY:
>But yes, we DO have something.

12 KINNEY/linked:
>And you're going to HATE it.

SEVEN:
CROCKER, waiting, annoyed, over-tired, under-fed, with a nicotine headache.

13 CROCKER:
>Well?

EIGHT:
Across the DESK, with the RED PHONE in FG, KINNEY indicating it. From his position at the side of the desk, CROCKER looking at the phone, to see what is being indicated.

14 KINNEY:
>Your MINDERS in their PIT?

Page 20

ONE:
In the PIT, KITTERING, WALLACE, and CHACE working
at their desks, reading either off their monitors
or out of files.

WALLACE and CHACE are both smoking.

NO COPY.

TWO:
Shot across WALLACE'S DESK, ECU of the RED PHONE
as he reaches for it.

1 SFX: dreet dreet

THREE:
Angle past CHACE as she looks over at WALLACE,
serious and somewhat expectant. WALLACE holding
the phone to his ear.

2 WALLACE:
                Minder One.

FOUR:
Angle between KITTERING and CHACE, exchanging
looks, while WALLACE listens to the phone.

NO COPY.

FIVE:
OTS CHACE on WALLACE, hanging up the phone, brow
furrowed.

3 CHACE:
                You on your bike?

4 WALLACE:
                No…

SIX:
POV CHACE, WALLACE looking at her, slightly
confused.

5 WALLACE:
                …D. Ops wants you in his OFFICE.

SEVEN:
From behind CHACE'S DESK, she's exiting in BG,
WALLACE and KITTERING looking at one another,
wondering what the hell is going on.

NO COPY.

Page 21

ONE:
Exterior of the MI6 BUILDING, and we can see the damaged from the blast better now that it's daylight.

1 KATE/inside:
          Minder Two to see you, sir.

TWO:
Interior Crocker's Office, he's behind his desk, looking at the open door. KATE is stepping back as CHACE enters.

KINNEY is still in the same chair as before.

2 CROCKER:
          Roll her IN.

3 CHACE:
          Sir?

THREE:
OTS CHACE, KINNEY seated to her right, giving her a look-over.

CROCKER, behind his desk, is lighting a new cigarette.

4 CROCKER:
          Don't think you've met David Kinney. He's my OPPOSITE NUMBER at Five.

FOUR:
CROCKER tossing his lighter down as CHACE shakes KINNEY'S HAND, though KINNEY still hasn't risen.

5 CHACE:
          It's a pleasure, sir.

6 KINNEY:
          Well, we'll SEE about that.

7 CROCKER:
          You can SIT, Tara.

FIVE:
POV CHACE, looking at CROCKER, who has taken the lighter up again, and is worrying it in his hands, cigarette dangling.

NO COPY.

SIX:
STET Previous, but CROCKER is now looking up, at CHACE. Dead serious.

8 CROCKER:

> Our BROTHERS at Five know who
> gave us the EARLY wake-up this
> morning.

SEVEN:
CHACE turning to look at KINNEY, who is very
pleased with himself.

9 KINNEY:

> Group of RUSSIANS, used to work
> for a man named MARKOVSKY.

10 KINNEY/linked:

> Ring any BELLS?

Page 22

ONE:
OTS CHACE, looking to CROCKER for confirmation.

1 CROCKER:

> He knows ALL about it, Tara, don't
> worry.

TWO:
OTS KINNEY, CHACE, looking at him, stony-faced.

2 CHACE:

> I killed him.

THREE:
OTS CROCKER, KINNEY, pleased with himself, looking
at CROCKER. CHACE still looking at KINNEY.

3 KINNEY:

> Yes, you did.

4 KINNEY/linked:

> Quite DEFTLY, too, from what we've
> heard.

5 KINNEY:

> Problem is, Markovsky had MATES...

FOUR:
Past CHACE, as KINNEY and CROCKER continue.

6 KINNEY:

> ...a LOT of them.

7 CROCKER:

> Five says the Russians KNOW who
> PULLED the TRIGGER.

8 CROCKER/linked:

> They're after US in general, and
> YOU specifically.[24]

24. Back when Oni Press did their Summer Color Specials, I had the honor of working with Stan Sakai, the amazingly talented creator of Usagi Yojimbo, on a story for the anthology. The story was, I believe, six pages, and told how Markovsky's people discovered that it was Chace who had pulled the trigger on their man.

FIVE:
Angle past KINNEY, grinning, at CHACE, who is looking at CROCKER. CROCKER is returning her gaze.

9 KINNEY:

You're leaving out the BEST part, Paul.

SIX:
CU CHACE, expressionless, eyes slightly down. There's some reasonable fear.

10 KINNEY/off:

There's a BOUNTY on YOUR head, Ms. Chace…

SEVEN:
KINNEY, looking smug.

11 KINNEY:

…ONE MILLION U.S. for the head of MINDER TWO.

Page 23

ONE:
CROCKER is up and crossing to KINNEY, who is still seated.CHACE is motionless.

1 CROCKER:

Get out!

2 KINNEY:

We're NOT fini—

TWO:
CROCKER yanking KINNEY from the chair by the back of his collar.

3 CROCKER:

I ALWAYS knew you were BASTARD, David—

THREE:
CROCKER, opening the door to his office with one hand, propelling KINNEY through with the other. KATE is looking up in surprise.

5 CROCKER:

—I just didn't know you were a SADIST, as well.

FOUR:
CHACE, still as before, in chair, in FG, as CROCKER shuts the door and turns back.

NO COPY.

FIVE:
Stet previous, CROCKER coming around CHACE'S seat.
She's bringing her eyes back up level, now.

6 CHACE:
>   They want me to be BAIT.

7 CROCKER:
>   If they make a TRY at you they'll
>   EXPOSE themselves.

SIX:
OTS CHACE, CROCKER standing at his window, looking
out as he fishes another cigarette.

8 CROCKER:
>   Once they're in the OPEN, we can
>   TAKE them.

9 CROCKER:
>   Make   them   ANSWER   for   THIS
>   MORNING.

SEVEN:
CU CHACE, thinking.

10 CHACE:
>   Assuming I SURVIVE the TRY.

EIGHT:
ECU CROCKER, he won't look at her.

11 CROCKER:
>   Assuming.

Page 24

ONE:
Past CROCKER, still looking out the window.

CHACE in the chair.

NO COPY.

TWO:
OTS CROCKER, looking at CHACE. CHACE is honestly
curious.

1 CHACE:
>   Did you know Jill Baron or Albert
>   Cooper?

THREE:
POV CHACE, CROCKER, looking unhappy.

2 CROCKER:
>   Yes.   Couldn't   STAND   either   of
>   them.

25. "Janitor" is an Americanism. I should have used "Custodian," instead.

3 CROCKER:

But the JANITOR[25]... Ravi Diop...

FOUR:
CU CHACE, serious, listening. If she's surprised, it's not registering.

4 CROCKER:

...he was a NICE man.

FIVE:
OTS CROCKER, as CHACE rises.

NO COPY.

SIX:
CHACE in the doorway, looking back at us/ Crocker.

6 CHACE:

Tell KINNEY I'll start whenever he's READY.

Queen & Country Issue Three

Page 1

ONE:
Exterior, view of TARA'S HOME in South Kensington. It's night and raining. A couple CARS are parked on the street. Other townhouses flank Tara's, running the length of the block. Uniform brick structures mostly. An OLD MAN walks a DOG down the block, in BG. Other than that, it's pretty much silent and still, as this is an establishing shot.

CHACE is barely visible as a silhouette through one of her windows, moving in her kitchen.

1 TAILLESS/elec:
                    Still there, Rose[1]?

1. I used "Crow" and "Raven" as call-signs in issue 1, following a bird theme. Here I went with flowers. I was intentionally trying to make the call-signs as bland and, frankly, unimaginative, as possible. It seemed more realistic to me than using, say, "Cobra" and "Sexy Mommma" and others along those lines.

TWO:
Interior of TARA'S HOME in South Kensington. We're in the kitchen/dining area. This is a small townhouse, remember, so the space is somewhat cramped. Angle across the kitchen table, where Tara has finished eating her dinner-for-one. A HALF-EMPTY glass of JUICE is on the table, some crumbs, a small hand-held RADIO, and a PISTOL.

CHACE is moving away from the table, putting her dish in the sink, in BG.

2 TAILLESS/elec:
                    Still here, Tulip. See anything worth reporting?

3 TAILLESS/elec:
                    Not much...

THREE:
Angle on the RADIO and PISTOL. CHACE has returned to the table, picking up the GLASS, so we're basically looking at her mid-section.

4 TAILLESS/elec:
                    ...though the BIRD in three-ten might be worth watching if she CHANGES for BED...

FOUR:
CHACE taking the radio in one hand, the PISTOL now

tucked in her waist band, carrying her glass in
the other, heading for the sink.

5 TAILLESS/elec:
> …but I have to REPORT that, sadly,
> DAISY'S NEIGHBORS are all DAMN
> UGLY.

FIVE:
At the sink, CHACE has set the RADIO on the
sideboard, the glass in the sink, and is pulling a
cigarette from a pack with her teeth. It's unclear
if she's actually listening.
6 TAILLESS/elec:
> Well, you know what you DO, Rose.

7 TAILLESS/elec:
> You SPY on DAISY. Sure to get an
> EYEFUL that way.

SIX:
CU CHACE, as she lights her cigarette. An eyebrow
is arching. She's clearly listening.

8 TAILLESS/elec:
> Brilliant, Tulip.

9 TAILLESS/elec:
> Then DAISY kills ME, the RUSSIANS
> kill her…

SEVEN:
From the sink, CHACE, carrying the RADIO in one
hand, her cigarette still burning in the other,
her back to us, as she heads out of the kitchen.

10 TAILLESS/elec:
> …and you're suddenly HEAD of the
> SPECIAL SECTION.

11 TAILLESS/elec:
> Ah, you've seen through my CUNNING
> PLAN…

Page 2

ONE:
Living room of Tara's home, wide shot. Again, it's
a somewhat cramped space, papers and books and CD
jewel cases scattered about. A couple pictures
on the walls—though they are pretty much devoid
of sentiment. Maybe an old concert poster or two
(Elvis Costello or Joe Jackson, I'm thinking, but
I'm biased as hell[2]).

2. Meaning these are my music tastes, rather than Tara's.

CHACE is making for the couch, RADIO and cigarette
still with her.

1 TAILLESS/elec:
> …you REALIZE what that MEANS, of

course.

2 TAILLESS/elec:
>I DO, indeed...

TWO:
CHACE on the couch, on her back, the cigarette in her mouth, the RADIO on her stomach, the PISTOL still in her waist band. Her expression is kind of tense.

3 TAILLESS/elec:
>...it means it's TIME for a new PLAN.

4 CHACE/small:
>...it means it's time for a new plan.

THREE:
Stet previous, but now CHACE is holding her smoke up and away from her face, and has brought the RADIO up to speak to it.

5 CHACE:
>Tulip, Rose, it's Daisy.

6 CHACE/linked:
>Shut the BLOODY HELL up.

FOUR:
Stet previous, but CHACE has moved the RADIO away from her mouth, and is taking a drag off the cigarette.

NO COPY.

FIVE:
Stet previous, but CHACE has the RADIO back to her mouth, the cigarette again out of the way.

7 CHACE:
>Thank you.
8 CHACE/linked:
>Daisy out.

Page 3

ONE:
Exterior of the townhouse, and now it's late at night. The rain is still coming down.

The lights inside are out.

We're looking past a parked CAR in FG. KITTERING is slouched behind the wheel.

1 CAPTION/Chace:
                    I feel JUSTIFIED in a certain
                    TARTNESS of TONE.[3]

TWO:
Interior of Tara's bathroom, OTS/behind CHACE as
she splashes water on her face at the sink. She's
in a tank-top/undershirt and her panties—oops,
pardon me, I meant knickers—basically ready for
bed.

The RADIO and PISTOL are balanced on the side of
the sink.

2 CAPTION/Chace:
                    I am, after all, worth one MILLION
                    dollars.

THREE:
Stet previous, Chace looking at her reflection. She
looks a little haggard, a little tired. A little
ill, as if she's been puking up her guts off an on
for a while now.

3 CAPTION/Chace:
                    Or at least, that's what the RED
                    MAFIYA is willing to PAY for my
                    head.

FOUR:
Close, as CHACE comes past us out of the bathroom,
switching off the light. The RADIO and PISTOL are
now on the nightstand.

4 CAPTION/Chace:
                    Not REALLY the same thing, is it?

FIVE:
Angle from above, as CHACE collapses onto her
bed.

5 CAPTION/Chace:
                    One wonders how they go about
                    making THAT particular request.

6 CAPTION/Chace:
                    Wanted: SIS Officer Tara Chace's
                    HEAD, preferably on PLATTER…

SIX:
Past the nightstand, RADIO, PISTOL visible, to
a CU of CHACE, looking at us, her head on her
pillow. She looks tense and tired.

7 CAPTION/Chace:
                    …BODY optional….

SEVEN:
Stet previous, but she's closed her eyes.

NO COPY.

3. We made it through the second issue
without resorting to Tara's narrative, but
I fell back upon it here, for a couple of
reasons, none of them very good. Mostly,
I was afraid I'd lost the reader, and that
someone picking up the book wouldn't
have the first clue what was going on.
For that reason, Tara's narrative here is
entirely expository, and that's just Bad
Writing, in my book. It doesn't really
forward the action, and what it reveals
about her personality is just as evident in
the visuals, in the "acting."
This was the moment, honestly, when I
realized that the first-person narrative
was inappropriate for the series, and that
it needed to go. I kept it through issue 4,
to maintain a manner of consistency, but
if I could do it again, I wouldn't bother
to even pretend. Steve's art was more
eloquent than any of my narrative, and
while I was able to turn a couple of cute
phrases here and there, that's pretty
much all I got out of it. I look at it now,
and I cringe, the same way I cringe when
I hear Harrison Ford's narration in Blade
Runner. It's unnecessary, and it insults the
audience by presuming that the audience
isn't smart enough to figure out what's
going on in the story.
I firmly believe that's insulting, and I
just as firmly believe in not insulting
my audience.

Pages 4 and 5

[*This is all MI6 office stuff, and should be laid out as functionally as possible, without becoming a boring grid. Maybe we can take a page from some of Bendis'[4] layouts when he gets dialogue heavy...*]

ONE:
Daylight, establishing of the MI6 building, with the BLAST DAMAGE visible from the previous issue. WORKMEN are repairing like nuts.

1 WALLACE/inside:
> ...sat on her ALL NIGHT and there was NO SIGN of anything...

TWO:
Interior of Crocker's Office, from behind Crocker's desk. CROCKER is standing, back to us, shrugging out of his overcoat. His focus is on the PAPERS on his desk.

WALLACE, looking rumpled, is in the doorway.

KATE is trying to edge past with two cups of coffee.

2 WALLACE:
> ...Ed's watching her place NOW.

3 CROCKER:
> You get any sleep?

4 WALLACE:
> As you know, I am a MASTER of the art of WANG-O-WANG which allows one to SLEEP with his eyes OPEN.

5 WALLACE/linked:
> I even DREAMED. Some of them were DIRTY. Want to hear one, boss?

THREE:
New angle, KATE setting the first cup on the desk, as CROCKER, still staring at his papers, flips through a couple. WALLACE is watching KATE with a slight grin.

6 CROCKER:
> You're about HALF the wit you think you are, Tom.[5]

7 CROCKER/linked:
> What about Minder Two?

8 WALLACE:
> Lights went off at TWENTY-THREE HUNDRED, about—

FOUR:
OTS WALLACE, taking the cup of coffee from KATE

This is the only thumbnail I could find from #3. As you can see, this was drawn before I realized it was two pages worth + Greg had just left the page break up to me. It sure felt like too many panels. I guess it pays to read the script more closely!

Steve

as she heads towards us, out of the office. CROCKER in BG is looking up with a scowl, having seen the exchange of smiles.

9 WALLACE:
      —thanks Kate—

10 WALLACE/linked:
      —what Tara did AFTER that, I've no clue.

11 CROCKER:
      Not much bloody USE, are you?

12 CROCKER/linked:
      KATE!

FIVE:
OTS CROCKER, as WALLACE jerks back in the doorway, trying to keep coffee from spilling on himself. KATE has turned around to look at Crocker, attentive.

13 KATE:
      Paul?

14 CROCKER:
      Did you call CHENG?[6]

6. And miraculously, Franks is Angela Cheng. For those who are interested in Easter Eggs and that kind of thing, Angela Cheng-Caplan is one of the two agents who represents my work (she handles the film rights and the like; my other agent, David Hale Smith, handles my literary work, and about a thousand other things). The character of Angela Cheng, CIA Station Chief, London, is based entirely on Angela Cheng, the Agent. This should give you a good sense of what she's like as an agent, and why I am devoted to her.

15 KATE:

Of course I did.

16 CROCKER:

And?

17 KATE:

And she'll be FREE after ONE this
afternoon.

18 CROCKER:

Not BEFORE?

SIX:
From the ante-room, Kate's office, as KATE comes
towards us. WALLACE in BG, looking after her with
a grin, and CROCKER fuming at the desk in EBG.

19 KATE:

No. Not before.

SEVEN:
CROCKER glaring after Kate, who is out of sight.
WALLACE is now grinning at CROCKER.

20 CROCKER:

I should FIRE her.

21 WALLACE:

Do that and you'll DESTROY us
all.

EIGHT:
Past WALLACE, sipping his coffee, as CROCKER drops
into his chair.

22 CROCKER:
                    Despite what KATE would have you
                    believe, TOM, she does NOT run the
                    Service.

23 WALLACE:
                    You're just cranky because Russians
                    are trying to kill your GIRL.

NINE:
Two-shot, CROCKER just shooting pure venom at
WALLACE.

WALLACE grinning.

NO COPY.

TEN:
Stet previous.

24 CROCKER:
                    I should have sent YOU to Kosovo.

25 WALLACE:
                    Yeah, probably. But I would've
                    MISSED the shot on Markovsky, and
                    then where would we be?

ELEVEN:
CROCKER has his head down, going through the
files in front of him. WALLACE is heading out the
door.

26 CROCKER:
                    Go get some sleep, then relieve
                    Ed.

27 WALLACE:
                    You COMMAND and I OBEY.

Page 6

ONE:
View of the CLOCK on the wall above Kate's
Desk. It's reading three minutes to one in the
afternoon.

1 KATE/below:
                    Paul! You're going to be LATE.

TWO:
Pull back, and we see that KATE is leaning on her

desk, head turned to CROCKER'S open office door.

CROCKER is emerging, pulling on his overcoat.

2 CROCKER:
> Call the Embassy, tell her I'll be
> in the PARK.

3 KATE:
> She's probably already LEFT—

4 CROCKER:
> She hasn't LEFT, she's running
> LATE, too.

THREE:
OTS KATE, as CROCKER heads out the door to the
ante-room, just as WELDON is coming in.

5 CROCKER:
> And when Minder Three gets in,
> tell him I'll see him when I get
> BACK—

6 WELDON:
> Paul.

FOUR:
CROCKER and WELDON. WELDON is trying to be
pleasant. CROCKER looks seriously annoyed.

7 CROCKER:
> Sir.

8 WELDON:
> Heading out?

9 CROCKER:
> Meeting with Cheng.

FIVE:
From the ante-room doorway, as WELDON moves past
KATE'S DESK, into CROCKER'S OFFICE.

CROCKER has turned in absolute frustration to
follow him.

KATE, at the desk, is looking sympathetic, and
reaching for the phone.

10 WELDON:
> A minute in your OFFICE, please.

SIX:
Tight, as WELDON enters the office. CROCKER
glowering at him.

NO COPY.

SEVEN:

Past CROCKER, as he goes back to his office. KATE
is already on the phone.

11 CROCKER:
                    Kate?

12 KATE:
                    I'll let her know.

Page 7

ONE:
From Crocker's desk, WELDON standing in the middle
of the office, CROCKER shutting the door behind him
as he enters.

NO COPY.

TWO:
Pretty much stet on the angle, WELDON hasn't
moved, CROCKER coming past him, not looking at
Weldon.

1 WELDON:
                    I saw a MEMO from MATERIEL this
                    morning about THREE Walther P99s.[7]

2 WELDON/linked:
                    Did you ARM the Minders?

3 CROCKER:
                    Chace is being hunted by THUGS in
                    the middle of LONDON, sir...

THREE:
CROCKER has stopped at his desk, not yet traveling
behind it. WELDON is looking at his back. WELDON
is on the verge of losing patience, but isn't
there yet. CROCKER looks frustrated, pulling a
cigarette from a pack on the desk.

4 CROCKER:
                    ...of COURSE I armed the MINDERS.

5 WELDON:
                    I can't have S.I.S. running about
                    LONDON like extras from some
                    American ACTION film, Paul.

FOUR:
OTS WELDON, CROCKER with a cigarette dangling,
just about to light it. His eyes are very dark—
he's not fucking about.

6 WELDON:
                    You get away with THAT behavior on
                    STATION, not at HOME.

7 WELDON/linked:
                    And certainly NOT when KINNEY and

7. I chose this weapon for no other
reason than that I like the gun. Apparently
I'm not the only one; it's the gun James
Bond is now using in the films.

                    the rest of FIVE breathing down
                    our necks.

FIVE:
WELDON, making a pinched face. He understands why
Paul did it, but he can't let it stand.

8 WELDON:
                    You have to DISARM them.

SIX:
WELDON and CROCKER. CROCKER is frustrated. WELDON
is calm, almost matter-of-fact.

9 CROCKER:
                    And when the Russians make their
                    TRY, what is Chace supposed to
                    DO?

10 CROCKER/linked:
                    Bat her EYES and ask them SWEETLY
                    to not MURDER her TOO MUCH?

SEVEN:
OTS CROCKER, WELDON starting to turn for the door.
He really does understand the problem.

11 WELDON:
                    I'm NOT saying it'll be EASY.

12 WELDON/linked:
                    But Wallace, Chace, and Kittering
                    comprise your SPECIAL SECTION...

EIGHT:
CU on CROCKER, just shy of snarling. Really
unhappy, angry, frustrated. Just generally a guy
who rarely ever smiles. Right now, he'd like to
kill someone, but he doesn't know who to blame—
Weldon's right, and he hates him for that.

13 WELDON/off:
                    ...perhaps it's TIME they PROVE how
                    SPECIAL they ARE.[8]

8. This line is one of the many I've stolen
from Ian Mackintosh over the course of
the series. It works so well, I used it in the
first Q&C novel, as well.

Page 8

ONE:
Interior of Chace's home, we're looking at the floor in the doorway to her bedroom. The RADIO and GUN are on the floor.

CHACE'S KNEES and FEET are hanging in panel—she's doing pull-ups, but we'll see that in a couple of panels. Right now we're going to be artsy-fartsy. She's got her knees bent so her feet are crossed at 90 degrees, parallel to the floor, behind her.

NO COPY.

TWO:
Stet previous, but now there's no sign of Tara.

NO COPY.

THREE:
Stet panel one.

NO COPY.

FOUR:
Stet panel two.

1 TAILLESS/elec:
        Daisy? It's TULIP…

FIVE:
Pull-back, still framed by the doorway. CHACE has dropped from the pull-up bar in the doorway. She's in jeans and a t-shirt, perspiring. She's been doing a lot of these. She is reaching for the RADIO.

2 TAILLESS/elec:
        …your PHONE is about to RING.

3 SFX: brrt brrt

SIX:
Stet angle, but now CHACE has taken the GUN and RADIO from the floor, and is moving into BG, back to us, heading for the phone on the nightstand. CHACE is speaking into the radio.

4 CHACE:
        That was very CLEVER, Tulip.

5 CHACE/linked:
        Can you tell me what happens next week on *Holby City*?[9]

9. Holby City is a spin-off of Casualty, which in turn was the BBC's take on ER.

6 TAILLESS/elec:
        Sorry.

7 SFX: brrt brrt

SEVEN

Stet angle, but now CHACE is answering the phone
in the BG.

8 CHACE:
>   Chace.

9 CROCKER/phone:
>   Tara? It's Paul.

10 CHACE:
>   Yes, sir?

EIGHT:
Stet previous, but CHACE'S posture has changed,
head now down.

11 CROCKER/phone:
>   I just had a meeting with the
>   Deputy Chief.

12 CROCKER/phone/linked:
>   He's ORDERED the Minders to turn
>   in their WEAPONS.

ONE:
CU on CHACE, on the phone. Serious expression.
She's thinking that the Deputy Chief has probably
just guaranteed she'll be dead soon.

NO COPY.

TWO:
Stet.

10. Steve, it turned out, was brilliant at these kinds of pages. I can't put my finger on exactly what it is he does, but he managed—time and again over these four issues—to bring an incredible emotional weight to the moments of stillness. Given that Steve got a lot of critical heat at the start of the series for his art style—he was called "too cartoony" by several different "critics" in several different forums, I think this gives proof to their lies.

Of interest, perhaps, is the fact that Steve was only the first to get this treatment. Throughout the series, each artist has had the pleasure of being unfavorably compared to the one who preceded him/her. This lasts until a new artist comes on the book, and then the last guy or gal is suddenly the Best Q&C Artist Ever.

1 CROCKER/phone:
        Ed will collect your gun when Tom
        replaces him.

2 CHACE:
        Very good, sir.

THREE:
Stet. CHACE has closed her eyes.

3 CROCKER/phone:
        I'm meeting with CHENG.

4 CROCKER/phone/linked:
        We'll come up with SOMETHING,
        don't worry.

5 CHACE:
        Yes, sir.

FOUR:
Stet, eyes still closed.

6 SFX/phone: klik

FIVE:
Across the bed, as CHACE hangs up the phone.

NO COPY.

SIX:
CHACE, sitting on the bed, RADIO and GUN next
to her. Her posture is tense and somewhat
depressed.

NO COPY.

SEVEN:
Stet, but CHACE is looking down at the RADIO.

7 TAILLESS/elec:
        Daisy? It's ROSE.

8 TAILLESS/elec/linked:
        Tulip's on his WAY to the door...

Pages 10 and 11

ONE:
This is the big image, spanning two pages.
Across the top and bottom run panels Two through
Thirteen.

Exterior of Hyde Park, day. Gray and overcast.
People walk with umbrellas. Nannies push prams.
Just what you'd expect. Some people are jogging.
But it is a beautiful park in the middle of
London.

CHENG and CROCKER, small, are walking side by side.
Each walks with their hands in their pockets.

ANGELA CHENG, for the record, is the CIA Station
Chief in London, based out of the Embassy in
Grosvenor Square. She's about a foot shorter than
Crocker, better dressed and better paid, and still
looks over-worked and over-tired. Her hair is
shoulder length. She's Chinese-American.

NO COPY.

TWO:
This is a side shot, upper bodies, of CROCKER
and CHENG, walking side by side, talking. CROCKER
should be in FG, closer to the camera. They rarely
look at one another as they talk, mostly watching
what's happening around them.

1 CHENG:
> You're the ONLY man I let keep me
> WAITING.

2 CROCKER:
> You let your AMBASSADOR keep you
> waiting.

3 CHENG:
> Actually, I DON'T.

THREE:
Stet previous, minor changes in posture. Perhaps
a breeze blows some of Cheng's hair.

4 CHENG:
> What happened?

5 CROCKER:
> Weldon wanted a PIECE of me.

6 CROCKER/linked:
> Doesn't like the Minders going
> ARMED in London.

FOUR:
Stet, again, minor changes.

7 CHENG:

> Can't say I BLAME him. They start SHOOTING, everyone on your FLOOR will need to update a resume.

8 CROCKER:

> Oh, I know he's CORRECT, Angela.

9 CROCKER/linked:

> I just wish he wasn't so damn SMUG about it.

FIVE:
Stet, again, minor changes.

10 CHENG:

> Is that what you wanted to meet about?

11 CROCKER:

> No, but it makes this more PRESSING.

12 CROCKER/linked:

> You know the situation?

SIX:
Stet previous, but CROCKER is actually looking at CHENG.

13 CHENG:

> Red Mafiya wants Chace's HEAD because of what she did to Markovsky.

SEVEN:
Now on the bottom row, and here we reverse, so that CHENG is in FG, CROCKER in BG, but postures and layout as above.

14 CROCKER:

> Should I even ASK how you KNOW?

15 CHENG:

> I'm CIA. We know EVERYTHING.[11]

EIGHT:
Stet previous, slight changes. CHENG is grinning. CROCKER is not.

16 CROCKER:

> Like you knew about AMES.[12]

17 CHENG:

> No fair! You didn't know about Philby, Maclean, Burgess—

18 CROCKER:

> Point taken.

11. They don't, actually, as George Tenent recently explained to the 9-11 Commission.

12 Aldrich "Rick" Ames was a CIA Intelligence Officer arrested in 1994 along with his wife for spying for the Soviets. Ames' arrest lead, in turn, to the revelation that, like the British, the KGB had succeeded in recruiting several double-agents in the U.S.. This came as quite a shock to a great many, who had thought the CIA untouched by such deceptions. It's thought that Ames betrayal cost the lives of at least 10 agents who were executed by the Soviets, as well as the compromise of some 100 separate intelligence operations. Ames worked in the Counterintelligence Division at the CIA, where he was responsible for—wait for it—directing analysis of Soviet intelligence operations.

QUEEN & COUNTRY SCRIPTBOOK

<u>NINE:</u>
Stet previous, slight changes, both now serious,
though.

19 CROCKER:
                    Can you help?

20 CHENG:
                    Help how?

21 CROCKER:
                    Give me some back-up.

<u>TEN:</u>
Stet, again with the slight changes. CHENG is
frowning, brow furrowed.

22 CHENG:
                    Don't you have Five backing you?
                    What's his name? Kinney?

23 CROCKER:
                    David Kinney, yes, and that's NOT
                    the HELP I'm looking for.

24 CROCKER/linked:
                    Kinney wants an ARREST.

<u>ELEVEN:</u>
Stet, again, still walking. CHENG is now looking
at CROCKER, vaguely alarmed. CROCKER is ignoring
the look.

25 CROCKER:
                    I want them DEAD.

26 CHENG:
                    Jesus Christ, Paul!

<u>TWELVE:</u>
Stet, both now walking without looking at each
other, thinking.

NO COPY.

<u>THIRTEEN:</u>
Stet, but now CHENG has stopped, and CROCKER is
moving out of panel.

27 CROCKER:
                    They ATTACKED us in our HOME,
                    Angela.

Page 12

<u>ONE:</u>
Still in the park. We're OTS CHENG, now looking
at CROCKER who has taken a bench and is pulling
out a cigarette.

NO COPY.

TWO:
CHENG sitting next to CROCKER. CROCKER is lighting
his cigarette. CHENG is thoughtful, watching the
pedestrians.

1 CROCKER:
> Can you help?

2 CHENG:
> What do I look like, Lady
> Macbeth?

THREE:
From behind the bench, both seated. CHENG is
leaning back. CROCKER is now leaning forward,
elbows on thighs.

3 CROCKER:
> One of MY people is being HUNTED
> because of a FAVOR I did the CIA.

4 CROCKER/linked:
> Chace took Markovsky at Langley's
> request.

FOUR:
Side shot, past CHENG in FG, CROCKER still leaning
forward, now glancing at her, vaguely hopeful.
CHENG is almost stern.

5 CHENG:
> For which Langley is GRATEFUL.

6 CHENG/linked:
> But they're not grateful enough
> to allow me to authorize a COVERT
> action in downtown London.

7 CROCKER:
> You could ASK.

FIVE:
CHENG looking at CROCKER with some frustration.
He's looking kinda depressed now.

8 CHENG:
> I KNOW what they'll say. They'll
> say NO.

9 CHENG/linked:
> And with GOOD reason. Can you
> imagine the political SHITSTORM
> we'd be in if anything LEAKED?

SIX:
Past CROCKER, who is now looking off into the
middle-distance, drawing on his cigarette.

CHENG is adjusting her hair, frowning.

10 CHENG:

> Forget the MIRROR, it'd be in the Washington Fucking POST.

11 CHENG/linked:

> No way the NEW President will let THAT happen. His position is TOO SHAKY right now.[13]

SEVEN:
Narrow horizontal band, CHENG and CROCKER on the bench.

NO COPY.

13. Truth, baby, is far stranger than any fiction of which I can conceive.
I believe this line was written before the results of the 2000 "election," hence the vagueness of the 'new President' line.

Page 13

ONE:
Looking past a ROMANTIC COUPLE in FG, as they walk with their arms around each other.

In BG, CROCKER and CHENG seated at the bench. CROCKER is leaning back.

1 CROCKER:

> All right, if you can't give me PERSONNEL, can you give EQUIPMENT?

2 CHENG:

> If you're going to say what I THINK you're going to say…

TWO:
CROCKER watching the ROMANTIC COUPLE pass by in the BG. CHENG is glaring at him, though she is, perhaps, amused at his lunacy.

3 CROCKER:

> Three PISTOLS, doesn't matter the MAKE, as long as they WORK.

4 CHENG:

> Hell no. Company GUN or Company GUNMAN, it's the SAME problem, Paul!

5 CROCKER:

> You have UNTRACEABLE weapons.

THREE:
CHENG, almost flopping back, exasperated. CROCKER is examining his burning cigarette.

6 CHENG:

> For use by OUR people, not YOURS.

7 CROCKER:

> So you've got NOTHING for me?

FOUR:
CHENG looking at CROCKER, annoyed. CROCKER is
flicking his butt away.

8 CHENG:

Only more verbal DARTS.[14]

9 CROCKER:

Sadly, Chace isn't in a position
to PLAY games.

14. Not sure how many—if any—people picked up on this, but Cheng's line here, and the one that follows, were very deliberate. She's suggesting to Crocker that, if he can't get real guns, use fake ones. A suggestion he follows.

FIVE:
On the bench, as CHENG rises, adjusting her
overcoat. CROCKER is frowning off in the distance,
barely listening, now.

10 CHENG:

Well, it might get her out of her
FLAT. And KIDS always have the
best toys.

11 CHENG/linked:

I've got to get back to the
Embassy.

12 CROCKER:

Yes.

SIX:
Longshot, as CHENG walks away, leaving CROCKER on
the bench.

13 CHENG:

Good luck with it.

Page 14

ONE:
CROCKER walking out of the park, distance shot.
He's in a foul mood.

NO COPY.

TWO:
CROCKER on a London street, passing shops. Head
down, deep in thought, scowling.

NO COPY.

THREE:
Side shot, as CROCKER passes a COMIC STORE, where
there are displays. Appropriate SUPER HERO garbage
in the windows, some ACTION FIGURES and DOLLS, and
a couple of discreetly placed PELLET GUNS.

He's not paying any attention.

NO COPY.

<u>FOUR:</u>
Stet previous, of the COMIC STORE WINDOW, with the
DISPLAY, Crocker is out of shot.

NO COPY.

<u>FIVE:</u>
Stet previous, but CROCKER is back, his back to
us, looking into the window.

NO COPY.

<u>SIX:</u>
From the street, CROCKER stepping into the
store.

NO COPY.

Page 15

<u>ONE:</u>
Exterior of the MI6 building. Afternoon. Repair
work continues on the blast damage.

1 CROCKER/inside:
     Kate!

<u>TWO:</u>
CROCKER entering the ante-room to his office,
carrying a SHOPPING BAG. KATE is springing up
behind her desk, alarmed.

2 KATE:
     Paul?

3 CROCKER:
     Where's Minder Three?

<u>THREE:</u>
Angle from the doorway to Crocker's office,
as CROCKER drops the SHOPPING BAG on Kate's
DESK, already heading our way, pulling off his
overcoat.

KATE is uncertain whether she should look in the
bag or follow him.

4 KATE:
     He's in the PIT, has been for over
     an HOUR now. PAUL—

5 CROCKER:
     Good, make sure he doesn't LEAVE.

6 CROCKER/linked:
     Actually, don't, I'll CALL him.

<u>FOUR:</u>
Angle on KATE, looking into the bag with some
trepidation, arching an eyebrow.

7 KATE:

        Paul, David Kinney—

8 CROCKER:

        RUN that down to DESIGN...

9 CROCKER/linked:

        ...tell them I want it by TONIGHT,
        and to make them look PROPER.

FIVE:
Inside Crocker's office, as CROCKER blows through
the door.

DAVID KINNEY is standing in front of the desk,
turning around to face him.

CROCKER is surprised—which translates to angry.

In BG, we can see that KATE has already taken up
the bag, and is looking at us through the doorway,
waiting for the rest of her instructions.

10 KATE:

        David Kinney is here to see you.

11 KINNEY:

        Paul.

SIX:
CU CROCKER, just scowling.

NO COPY.

SEVEN:
Past KINNEY, looking at CROCKER, who in turn is
glancing at KATE in BG.

12 CROCKER:

        Get it done.

13 KATE:

        Tonight, and proper.

Page 16

ONE:
In the office, CROCKER moving to his desk. KINNEY
is standing, watching him.

1 CROCKER:

        Hope you WERE waiting long.

2 KINNEY:

        Not VERY.

3 KINNEY/linked:

        What's the hold-up?

TWO:
Past the DESK, CROCKER'S HAND dropping his pack
of cigarettes. KINNEY looking at CROCKER, being
a hard-ass.

4 CROCKER/above:
                    Hold-up?

5 KINNEY:
                    Chace hasn't moved in TWO DAYS.
                    What are you WAITING for?

THREE:
CROCKER in his chair, looking at KINNEY with
barely hidden contempt. KINNEY is returning it.

6 CROCKER:
                    I want my people in place before
                    she goes under FIRE, if that's all
                    RIGHT.

7 KINNEY:
                    MY people are ALREADY in place.

FOUR:
Past KINNEY, CROCKER leaning forward and taking
a cigarette from his pack. He's not looking at
Kinney, and is perhaps mildly amused.

8 CROCKER:
                    Then you UNDERSTAND my FEARS.

FIVE:
CU KINNEY, getting ticked.

9 KINNEY:
                    I understand you're CODDLING her.
                    She stays INDOORS, the RUSSIANS
                    won't MOVE on her.

10 KINNEY/linked:
                    She's supposed to be DRAWING them
                    OUT.

SIX:
CROCKER, holding his lighter, but his eyes are on
KINNEY.

11 CROCKER:
                    And in TIME she will.

12 KINNEY:
                    Time we don't HAVE.

SEVEN:
Angle past CROCKER'S ELBOW, as he sets the lighter
back down. KINNEY is leaning forward, hands on
the desk.

13 KINNEY:
                    I want this DONE tonight.

14 KINNEY/linked:
>Order her into MOTION and quit STALLING.

Page 17

ONE:
Two-shot. CROCKER and KINNEY glaring at each other.

NO COPY.

TWO:
Stet, but KINNEY has straightened up, is adjusting his suit-coat.

1 KINNEY:
>Do I need to speak to WELDON?

2 CROCKER:
>Your NOSE does seem REMARKABLY free of SHITE.

3 CROCKER/linked:
>A quick VISIT couldn't HURT.

THREE:
OTS CROCKER, KINNEY almost livid.

4 KINNEY/small:
>right.

FOUR:
Angle as KINNEY leaves Crocker's office, nearly smashing into KATE as she comes around the corner to look in on Paul.

NO COPY.

FIVE:
In the doorway, KATE now looking after Kinney, off. CROCKER has joined her, eyebrow arched.

5 KATE:
>You're still MATES, I see.

6 CROCKER:
>Shut up.

7 CROCKER/linked:
>He's going to WELDON.

SIX:
On KATE, now looking after Crocker as he goes back into his office.

8 KATE:
>Why?

9 CROCKER/off:
> He's accusing me of CODDLING
> Chace...

SEVEN:
OTS KATE, CROCKER at the desk, standing, picking up the RED PHONE.

10 CROCKER:
> ...wants the DC to order me to order
> her to give the RUSSIANS their
> SHOT.

11 CROCKER/linked:
> What about the OTHER thing?

12 KATE:
> Ready by sixteen hundred.

EIGHT:
CU CROCKER on the phone.

13 CROCKER:
> Good.

14 CROCKER/linked:
> Ed? It's D. Ops. My OFFICE,
> please...

Page 18

ONE:
On the street outside Chace's home. It's night.

WALLACE is kneeling in FG, tying his shoe. He's stopped in front of one of the houses on the street. The house has a small alcove and the front door is within that. On the second floor of the building we can see that the curtains in the window have been slightly parted, and we can see a HAND adjusting them.

In WALLACE'S LEFT EAR, we can see the little RECEIVER for his radio, and a CABLE running down to his collar, disappearing inside his shirt.[15]

1 CHACE/elec/tailless:
> ...how many?

2 WALLACE/small:
> At least TWO, so DOUBLE that
> number.

3 WALLACE/small/linked
> Tulip there?

TWO:
Interior of Chace's place, with CHACE in BG, peering out her blinds discreetly. It's pretty

15. This is a fine example of Greg asking for too many things in a single panel, something I do with alarming frequency, I'm afraid. My philosophy when scripting for a comic essentially comes down to this—my panel descriptions are about 80% optional; I'm far more concerned with conveying to the artist the movement of the story: what is happening, why it matters, what the characters feel about it, what the theme, tone, and emotional intent is. Ideally, after reading one of my scripts, the artist knows what it is I'm trying to accomplish, and then can tailor his or her choices to that best effect. I'm not an artist; I've tried, God knows, but it's a sad sight to see me with a pencil and a sketchpad. I leave the visuals to the professionals, and I handle the words and the story, so to speak.

If you compare the script with the actual comic, the work that Steve did, he followed me very closely, perhaps to the story's detriment, because sometimes I make very bad choices. I'm not saying that this is one; I'm just saying that my visual sense is for shit for the most part. Steve's, thank God, isn't.

dark inside. She's on her RADIO.

In FG, back to us, is KITTERING, holding the SHOPPING BAG.

4 CHACE:
Just arrived.

5 WALLACE/elec/tailless:
I'll be right in, then.

THREE:
Two-shot, wide, as CHACE turns away from the window to face KITTERING. KITTERING is trying to be cheerful, but CHACE looks exhausted.

6 CHACE:
He's coming.

7 KITTERING:
Good.

8 CHACE:
You want a DRINK?

FOUR:
Past KITTERING, watching CHACE as she pours herself a Scotch from the bottle at the sideboard. She still holds the RADIO in one hand.

9 KITTERING:
Doesn't strike me as the TIME.

10 CHACE:
Me, either.

FIVE:
CHACE draining the glass.

KITTERING watching.

NO COPY.

SIX:
OTS CHACE, looking at the back door. KITTERING has turned to look, as well.

WALLACE is entering.

11 WALLACE:
Sorry about that.

12 KITTERING:
We're SURE it's them?

13 WALLACE:
Them or FIVE.

SEVEN:
CHACE putting her glass back down.

14 CHACE:
>It's them.

Page 19

ONE:
Angle on WALLACE, KITTERING, and CHACE in the living room. KITTERING has set the BAG on the coffee table, and is reaching inside.

1 WALLACE:
>So what is the GOOD WORD from Master Crocker?

2 KITTERING:
>He offers TOYS and INSTRUCTIONS.

3 KITTERING/linked:
>We're each to take one of THESE...

TWO:
Looking into the BAG as KITTERING lifts out a PELLET GUN, black, and a passable fake for a real gun is you don't look too hard at it.[16]

4 KITTERING/above:
>...and then watch Tara go for a WALK by the WATER.

THREE:
KITTERING handing PELLET GUNS to CHACE and WALLACE.

Both CHACE and WALLACE look almost expressionless, taking the weapons, looking at them.

5 WALLACE:
>Are these PELLET GUNS?

6 KITTERING:
>Yes. We're to BLUFF with them.

7 WALLACE:
>Bluff.

8 KITTERING:
>Yes.

9 KITTERING/linked:
>Gets WORSE. Kinney got the DC to ORDER Tara into the OPEN...

FOUR:
On CHACE, as she holds up the PELLET GUN, examining it. Again, almost no expression whatsoever.

10 KITTERING/off:
>...assured him that FIVE would provide ADEQUATE back-up.

16. This isn't as ludicrous as it may first appear; at the San Diego Comic Con for the last several years, there have been at least three dealers selling "fake" guns that fire hard plastic BBs. Apparently, you can use these things for paintball—a recreation I have never tried, myself—and target shooting. The guns are available in almost every common make and model available, and they look incredibly realistic. So realistic, in fact, that were you to wander around with one outdoors, there's a very good chance you'd get shot by a cop. The few that have safety orange pieces around the end of the barrel don't really do much to convince one that these are not the real thing.

The idea here was that, of course, Crocker had procured exactly these kinds of pistols.

FIVE:
KITTERING and WALLACE watching CHACE, as she looks
at the gun in her hand. It's pretty clear that
all of them are thinking that she's going to die
shortly, including her.

11 WALLACE:
>   Five wants ARRESTS. They'll try to
>   take the RUSSIANS alive.

12 KITTERING:
>   Which means they'll WAIT until
>   AFTER the try.

SIX:
Stet previous, but CHACE has lowered the PELLET
GUN, now looking off, to the window. Her expression
is still blank, resigned.

NO COPY

SEVEN:
Past WALLACE, as he and KITTERING watch CHACE head
into her bedroom.

13 CHACE:
>   I'll get my COAT.

Page 20

ONE:
Exterior of the house, night. We're OTS KITTERING,
watching from shadow.

CHACE is emerging from inside, well-illuminated
from above by her porch/door light. She's in her
coat, hands deep in pockets.

NO COPY.

TWO:
OTS WALLACE, opposite end of the block.

CHACE is small in BG, coming towards us slowly.

NO COPY.

THREE:
Almost a bird's-eye, from above the street. CHACE
walking alone on her side of the street.

KITTERING in SHADOW at the top of the street.

NO COPY.

FOUR:
From the doorway of the HOUSE WITH THE CURTAINS, TWO MEN are emerging slowly, looking after CHACE.

CHACE is at the end of the block, turning the corner. No sign of Kittering or Wallace.

NO COPY.

FIVE:
Angle along the street, as the TWO MEN move to catch up with Chace, now out of sight.

1 TAILLESS/elec:
            You've got TWO, Daisy.

2 TAILLESS/elec:
            Understood.

SIX:
Past WALLACE, watching the TWO MEN turn the corner. CHACE is in EBG. WALLACE is speaking into his radio.

Down the street where Tara's home is, we can see KITTERING approaching the doorway the two men emerged from.

3 WALLACE/small:
            Tulip, go.

SEVEN:
Tight past KITTERING, as he edges up to the doorway where the TWO MEN emerged.

In EBG, we see WALLACE is moving to follow the Two Men, who are now off.

4 KITTERING/very small:
            In motion.

Page 21

[*Greg's general note on violence: make this as savage and fast as possible, please. It should be nasty, it should be painful, it should be ugly. Thanks and have a nice day!*]

ONE:
Looking straight on at the doorway where the two men emerged. KITTERING is pressed against the wall beside the doorway, listening, waiting. Very tense. He has the PELLET GUN in his hand.

Another TWO MEN—these are all of the Russian Thug variety—are coming out the door.

NO COPY.

TWO:
OTS KITTERING, as the TWO RUSSIANS emerge. The FIRST is looking in the direction Chace and the others headed. The SECOND is turning to look in Kittering's direction. Both of them look confident and wary and willing to do violence.

NO COPY.

THREE:
KITTERING hits the SECOND RUSSIAN in the throat with the knuckles of his free hand. This is almost a karate style attack, though not a hi-ya thing.[17]

FIRST RUSSIAN, now slightly ahead, is reacting to this sudden noise and movement, trying to turn and pull a PISTOL at the same time.

NO COPY.

FOUR:
SECOND RUSSIAN has dropped to his knees, eyes wide, clutching at his throat. He's choking to death, because Kinney just cracked his trachea. If we can really see his expression, it's the look of a man who is suffocating.

KITTERING is striking the FIRST RUSSIAN alongside the head with the PELLET GUN.[18] The FIRST RUSSIAN has his hands tangled in his jacket, trying to free his gun.

NO COPY.

FIVE:
FIRST RUSSIAN going down on his knees in FG, blood streaming down the side of his face, as KITTERING bashes him again with the PELLET GUN.

In BG, SECOND RUSSIAN has collapsed, dying.

NO COPY.

17. Very deliberate. Kittering's strike to the throat is done to keep the man silent, as well as to put him down. He crushes the windpipe so no alarm can be raised.

18. You've probably seen pistol-whipping in far too many films to count. I try to avoid using that particular tactic, because nobody who actually relies on a firearm to keep themselves alive would ever use their weapon as a club; it's just not done. In this instance, of course, Kittering is using the gun as a hammer, because that's essentially all that it is.

Page 22

ONE:
KITTERING, sweating, breathless, on his radio. His eyes are dark. Ideally, this should be a somewhat disturbing panel, since KITTERING is the youngest and most innocent looking of the bunch. He's looking down at the bodies in front of him.

1 KITTERING:
                    Rose, Daisy. Two DOWN...

TWO:
Wide shot, KITTERING in front of the house, with the TWO RUSSIANS down.

2 KITTERING:
>   …I'll call HOME and have them
>   COLLECTED…

THREE:
CU CHACE, walking towards us, hands still in her
pockets.

In BG, we can see the TWO MEN are following her,
about 100 feet back. We're walking down towards
the Thames, now, and the architecture should
reflect that.

The streets are empty and quiet.

3 KITTERING/elec/tailless:
>   …the rest are yours.

4 CAPTION/Chace:
>   Two of them.

FOUR:
Wide shot, CHACE at one end of the panel, turning
to walk along the water.

The TWO MEN are in mid-panel, walking side-by-
side, heads canted together.

No sign of Wallace.

5 CAPTION/Chace:
>   Wallace and I can TAKE two of
>   them.

FIVE:
Close on the TWO MEN. One of them is looking in
Chace's direction, plotting murder.

The OTHER MAN is looking over his shoulder,
suspicious.

6 CAPTION/Chace:
>   Just pick the MOMENT.

Page 23

ONE:
OTS OTHER MAN, and there's no sign of Wallace. His
PARTNER is tapping him on the shoulder, gesturing
to a point off panel.

1 CAPTION/Chace:
>   Just don't PANIC.

TWO:
Down-angle, CHACE in FG, walking along the water.
In EBG, we see the TWO MEN splitting up, ONE
moving in closer on CHACE, the OTHER sprinting

into an alley.

2 CAPTION/Chace:
>   That's all it's about.

THREE:
CU CHACE, and we can see the tension on her face.

Over her shoulder, we can see the MAN still on her trying to nonchalantly close the distance.

3 CAPTION/Chace:
>   It's not about THEM. Croatia or Colombia...

4 CAPTION/Chace:
>   ...it's NEVER about them....

FOUR:
From above, and we see that CHACE is moving towards an alley that dumps into her path. CRATES or some other obstruction hides the opening from her view. It's all very secluded. The MAN following her is perhaps only twenty-five feet back, now.

6 CAPTION/Chace:
>   It's about the FEAR.[19]

19. I like that Tara feels fear. It humanizes her immensely, in my opinion, and it's one of the things that grounds the series in reality.

FIVE:
Angle, past the opening of the alley. CHACE is coming towards us. Very tense. The MAN behind her is closing.

In FG, coming into the opening that CHACE is heading for, is the OTHER MAN. OTHER MAN has a GUN in his hand.

7 CAPTION/Chace:
>   Wait.

8 CAPTION/Chace:
>   Wait.

ONE:
Tight CU CHACE, painfully aware of the MAN closing behind her.

Over her shoulder, we see the MAN moving in, looking grim, ready to produce a gun of his own.

1 CAPTION/Chace:
                    Wait…

2 CAPTION/Chace:
                    …closer…

3 CAPTION/Chace:
                    …closer…

TWO:
From behind the MAN who has been following CHACE, as he stops, startled, drawing his gun.

CHACE has spun around, drawing the PELLET GUN and bringing it up in both hands.

There's at least 20 feet between them.

4 CAPTION/Chace:
                    …oh damn oh dammit too FAR…[20]

5 CHACE/big:
                    DROP IT! DROP IT—

THREE:
CHACE charging the MAN who has been following her, both hands holding the PELLET GUN, her face full of fury and adrenaline-fear.

The MAN is raising his GUN, refusing to be cowed.

In BG, the OTHER MAN is emerging, ready to shoot her.

6 CAPTION/Chace:
                    …not going to going to shoot close
                    the distance run close the distance
                    run RUN—

FOUR/FIVE/SIX:
POV CHACE, as the MAN fires at her three times. Set these up however you like—the same image with three gutters or the same image stet three times or whatever works.

7 SFX: BLAMM BLAMM BLAMM

20. From this range, the pellet/BB would have expended pretty much all of its energy reaching its target. This, tied to the fact that 20 feet is a fair distance to cover when someone is pointing a gun at you, are why Tara reacts as she does.
    I'm not particularly happy with the ending of this issue, as far as it goes. As with the narrative captions earlier this issue, I look back at this and think I'm crutching, that I was afraid I'd lose the reader if I didn't go out on something Very Big and Very Dramatic. Hence the firing sequence, which really is far more "tune in next week!" than I normally like for Queen & Country.

Queen & Country Issue Four

Page 1

ONE:
Overhead shot, horizontal, of the location from
the end of last issue, the MAN at the far left,
arm extended with gun in hand, firing at CHACE who
is charging him from the right. She's about 15
feet from the MAN.

From the far right, behind CHACE, the OTHER MAN
has emerged, raising his gun.

1 CAPTION/Chace:
　　　　　　There's a trick, they teach it to
　　　　　　you at the School.

2 CAPTION/Chace:
　　　　　　When someone pulls a GUN on you,
　　　　　　they say...

TWO:
POV CHACE, of the MAN, firing at her. He holds his
PISTOL in one hand, and he's squeezing off rounds
as fast as he can, an expression of determined
hate on his face.

3 CAPTION/Chace:
　　　　　　...CHARGE at him like a bloody
　　　　　　LUNATIC...

THREE:
POV MAN, still firing with CHACE just about on him.
CHACE still holds her PELLET GUN. A BULLET has
just torn through the shoulder of her jacket.

In EBG, past CHACE, we can see the OTHER MAN
falling.

4 CAPTION/Chace:
　　　　　　...it's the LAST thing they EXPECT
　　　　　　and most of them can't hit WATER
　　　　　　from a SUBMARINE anyway...

FOUR:
CHACE leaping.

5 CAPTION/Chace:
　　　　　　...and repeat to yourself OVER and
　　　　　　OVER that you're doing this for
　　　　　　QUEEN and COUNTRY.[1]

1. I actually have no idea if they teach this technique anywhere at all, but there are at least a couple of facts that support the theory that charging the shooter in this instance may be the best option. First, she has the element of surprise. Second, most of the folks—read, Bad Guys—don't know how to shoot; they've learned all their firearms technique from movies and television, and let me tell you, you fire a pistol "gangsta style," all you're doing is spraying lead. Third, most shooting instances are "uncontrolled," meaning that the weapon isn't fired in a moderated fashion; it's not squeeze, bang, squeeze, bang, but rather Ohmygod bangbangbangbangbangclickclickclick.

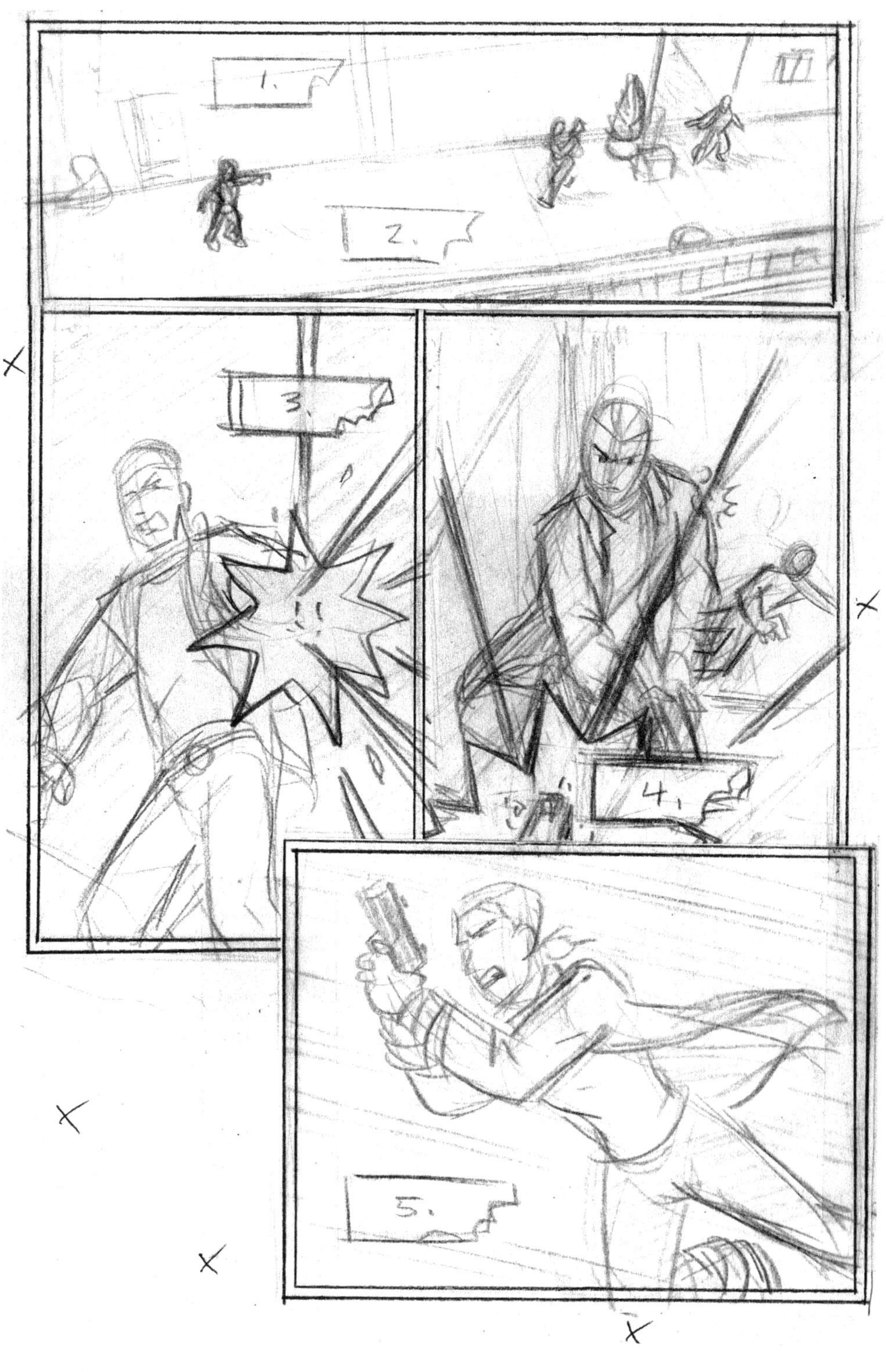
1.
2.
3.
4.
5.

ONE:
CHACE smashing into the MAN, forcing his gun arm
out and away, a final shot going wild.

NO COPY.

TWO:
CHACE and the MAN hitting the ground, with her
basically riding him down, in full flight-or-fight
mode with the switch taped to the 'fight' position.
One hand is on the MAN'S gun, twisting it out of
his grip, and with her other she is beating him
with the PELLET GUN.

NO COPY.

THREE:
CU CHACE grabbing the MAN'S GUN with one hand,
CLUBBING HIM with the PELLET GUN in the other.
There's blood.

NO COPY.

FOUR:
Angle, along the ground, looking at the top of
the MAN'S HEAD, CHACE basically astride him, now
pressing the PELLET GUN to the man's left eye.

WALLACE is approaching in BG, visible.

NO COPY.

FIVE:
Tight shot from the side, CHACE holding the PELLET
GUN to the MAN'S HEAD. The MAN, bloodied and
dazed, staring up at her. CHACE is breathless, her
hair wild, and she's ready to kill him.

WALLACE'S LEGS are in the panel, now, and he's
putting a hand on CHACE'S SHOULDER.

1 WALLACE/above:
            Tara.

SIX:
Stet previous.

NO COPY.

SEVEN:
Stet previous, CHACE now looking up at WALLACE.
She looks almost stunned.

4 WALLACE/above:
            It's DONE.

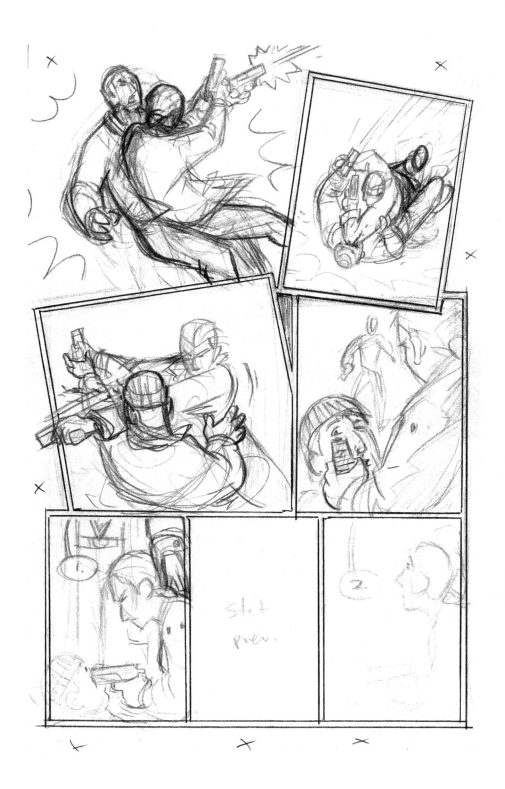

Page 3

ONE:
Wider, as WALLACE helps CHACE to her feet. She's unsteady.

1 CHACE:
>   There was ONE more.

2 WALLACE:
>   Yeah, he's NOT going to be TROUBLE.

TWO:
Past the OTHER MAN, who on the ground by the mouth of the alley, on his back, dead. A pool of blood is spreading beneath him.

In BG, CHACE and WALLACE are looking at him.

3 WALLACE:
>   One of the ROUNDS that missed you FOUND him.

4 CHACE/small:
>   Christ.

5 WALLACE:
>   It's HOLLYWOOD what does it, you ask me.

6 WALLACE/linked:
>   These blokes see a MOVIE where everyone's prancing about, firing CANNONS with one HAND...

THREE:
Tight on WALLACE and CHACE. CHACE is still semi-dazed, staring at the corpse, off.

WALLACE is crouching down over the MAN, searching him.

7 WALLACE/off:
>   ...they're more concerned with looking GOOD during a gunfight than with LIVING through the damn thing.

FOUR:
CHACE fumbling out her cigarettes. Still the same expression.

8 WALLACE/off:
>   What they don't REALIZE, you see, is that EVERY bullet has to go SOMEWHERE.[2]

2. A personal pet peeve, but I hate it in film or television when I see a gunfight where the bullets that miss just disappear into the ether. They don't. They hit something, sooner or later, and sometimes, it's something that has a pulse.

FIVE:
CU CHACE, noticing the BULLET HOLE, almost a curious expression.

NO COPY.

SIX:
CHACE poking her finger through the hole, and it comes out the other side.

9 CHACE:

> Hey… Tom?

10 WALLACE:

> Yes, love?

SEVEN:
WALLACE looking up from where he's pulling the MAN to his feet, but not at CHACE, rather past her and off panel.

CHACE is just looking at him kind of thoughtfully.

11 CHACE:

> …nothing.

12 CHACE/linked:

> Never mind.[3]

13 WALLACE:

> Ah, good Master Kinney and Etcetera have ARRIVED.

3. Violence is random by nature, yet another theme of the series. It doesn't care where it falls, and you can do everything right, and still die, and do everything wrong, and still live. Nothing, in my experience, more typifies this fact than a bullet. They're terribly unpredictable creatures, even before they enter a human body; the second the hit something—anything—a million factors come into play upon them. And when a bullet entires a body, all bets are off. They bounce and twist and ricochet and rebound. They make little holes the size of a pen cap, and big holes the size of a cantelope. They tear and rip and puncture and slice. They are vicious little creatures.

The fact that this mystery bullet hole appears goes to that point—clearly, Tara was closer to dying than even she realized. Where'd it come from? How'd it miss her? When did it happen? None of it matters.

She almost died there, and she knows it. And there's really nothing anyone can say to that.

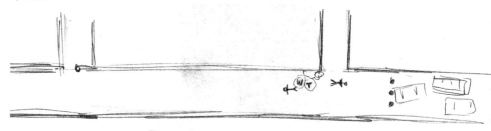

Page 4

ONE:
CHACE is lighting her cigarette, while WALLACE, now with the MAN on his feet, is looking past her into the BG, where we can see the flashing lights of a couple POLICE CARS have stopped, their doors open. An UNMARKED CAR is also present.

KINNEY and a couple of CONSTABLES run towards her from the BG.

1 KINNEY:

> What the HELL happened here?

TWO:
Angle on CHACE as KINNEY storms up behind her. KINNEY is furious. CHACE is closing her lighter, trying to keep her mouth shut.

CONSTABLES are moving past the two of them like they're a rock in the middle of a stream of police.

2 KINNEY:
> You! CHACE!

3 KINNEY/linked:
> I want an ANSWER, by GOD!

THREE:
Angle past WALLACE in FG, handing over the MAN to a pair of CONSTABLES.

KINNEY, past them, is now behind CHACE, who is stowing her lighter, and looking at WALLACE with an expression that says she'd happily kill Kinney if only she thought she could get away with it.

4 KINNEY:
> You stupid BITCH!

5 KINNEY/linked:
> Your ORDERS were to draw them OUT, NOT to ENGAGE!

FOUR:
Tighter, with KINNEY fuming beyond CHACE'S shoulder—and of course it is the shoulder with the bullet hole.

6 KINNEY:
> I KNEW Crocker would try something like THIS—

Page 5

ONE:
CHACE has rounded on KINNEY, and her look is pure savage venom, barely contained. It's taking Kinney by surprise.

1 KINNEY:
> —turning his THUGS loose to pursue a VENDETTA—

2 CHACE:
> MISTER Kinney!

TWO:
KINNEY taking a step back, as CHACE gets in his face. She's taller than him, she's got some blood spattered on her face, she's had a rotten fucking week, and she knows eleven different ways to kill him.

KINNEY seems to be realizing all of these things, too.

NO COPY.

THREE:
Stet, but CHACE is pushing him out of her way, preparing to go past.

3 CHACE:
SOD fucking OFF.

THREE:
Past KINNEY, turning to see CHACE already moving away. WALLACE is moving to follow her, just passing KINNEY with a small smile and nod.

4 CHACE:
You have a PROBLEM with my PERFORMANCE, you're free to take it up with my D. OPS…

FOUR:
Behind KINNEY in FG, watching as WALLACE catches up to CHACE.

In BG, COPS are moving around the corpse of the OTHER MAN. Lights continue to flash.

5 CHACE:
…at which point I'll be DELIGHTED to tell the HOME OFFICE about how you arrived just AFTER the nick of TIME.

FIVE:
Stet, but KINNEY is turning to face us, expression dark, very angry. In BG, CHACE and WALLACE are passing through the cops.

6 KINNEY/small:
Damn bitch.

4. Terms like "The Farm" and "The School" are stolen straight from LeCarré. "The School," as such, actually exists; it's Fort Monkton, in Gosport, near Portsmouth, and has been used as the SIS training facility for ages. I've heard rumors—and may have encountered a legitimate reference or two at some point, though I can't recall where—of an SIS debriefing facility somewhere in the Midlands, presumably "The Farm," though where it is, I don't know. Certainly, it's known that SIS maintains facilities throughout England for operational use. In his book, MI-6: Inside the Covert World of Her Majesty's Secret Intelligence Service, author Stephen Dorril references "cooler" facilities in Chelsea, as well as a sound-proofed "rubber room" which is, inexplicably, located in the basement of one of London's finer hotels. Both locations are apparently used for the interrogation and debriefing of "recalcitrant officers and agents under suspicion."

Page 6

ONE:
Exterior of MI-6, day. The repair work on the blast damage outside is nearly complete, now.

1 CROCKER/inside:
—to the FARM[4] for interrogation.

TWO:
Interior of Weldon's office. WELDON seated behind his desk, a cup of tea steaming in front of him. Morning light is streaming through the windows.

WELDON is king of his domain, very pleased with himself.

CROCKER stands in front of the desk, in his suit, giving his report. He's not quite so happy, but for once he doesn't look like he wants to staple anyone to anything.

He has a FOLDER beneath one arm, tucked.

2 CROCKER:
>They're under guard now, and Kinney has his QUESTIONERS en route.

3 WELDON:
>And the Minders?

THREE:
OTS WELDON, CROCKER continuing.

4 CROCKER:
>I sent them home after they filed their reports.

5 CROCKER/linked:
>Wallace and Chace will be back in the PIT on STAND-BY before NOON.

FOUR:
CU of the cup of tea, as WELDON squeezes a lemon wedge into the cup.

Perhaps a portion of CROCKER is visible.

6 WELDON/above:
>Not KITTERING?

7 CROCKER/off:
>Edward's with Doctor Callard[5], then OFF for the rest of the DAY.

FIVE:
WELDON, looking at Crocker/us with some surprise and some genuine concern.

8 WELDON:
>The report said NOTHING about Kittering taking an INJURY.

SIX:
CROCKER, respectful as he can be, thinking that Weldon's an idiot.

9 CROCKER:
>That's CORRECT, sir.

10 CROCKER/linked:
>He did, however, KILL one of the RUSSIANS with his BARE HANDS.

SEVEN:
WELDON taking his tea, more interested in its contents than in thinking about the hypocrisy of what he's saying. CROCKER watching.

11 WELDON:
>Ah, right.

5. Doctor Elizabeth Callard appears in the second arc, Operation: Morningstar. Again, this is an example of the 'logical extrapolation' game I play while writing. I have no direct sources indicating that SIS maintains a staff psychiatrist whose duties include the mental health and well-being of SIS Officers. But it seems to me, in a day and age where the NSA actually maintains a Gay/Lesbian/Bi Support Group for its personnel, that such a thing would not exist.
Whether or not an evaluation would be required as a matter of course after an agent kills in the line of duty is pure speculation, and probably unreasonable.

12 WELDON/linked:

    Well, he didn't have any CHOICE, did he, Paul?

13 CROCKER:

    No, sir.

Page 7

ONE:
OTS CROCKER, as WELDON sips his tea.

NO COPY.

TWO:
Stet, WELDON looking up at CROCKER in some surprise.

1 WELDON:

    Was there something ELSE, Paul?

2 CROCKER:

    What will happen to the Russians AFTER Five finishes their INTERROGATION?

THREE:
WELDON setting down his tea, still relatively happy, if minutely annoyed. CROCKER is as before, calm and somewhat complacent.

3 WELDON:

    Don't KNOW, to be honest, and don't much CARE.

4 WELDON/linked:

    EXTRADITION back to MOSCOW most likely.

5 WELDON:

    Why?

FOUR:
CROCKER offering WELDON the folder he's been carrying.

6 CROCKER:

    I'm looking for your APPROVAL on this.

7 WELDON:

    Is this IMMEDIATE?

FIVE:
WELDON taking the FOLDER, looking at CROCKER with curiosity.

8 CROCKER:

    Close of PLAY will be FINE, sir.

9 WELDON:
>   Very well.

10 WELDON/linked:
>   That'll be ALL for now.

SIX:
CROCKER almost out the door, stopping.

11 WELDON/off:
>   Paul!

12 CROCKER:
>   Sir?

SEVEN:
OTS CROCKER as he leans back into the office. WELDON at the desk, offering a very smarmy smile.

13 WELDON:
>   Congratulate the Minders for me.

14 WELDON/linked:
>   Job well done.

15 CROCKER:
>   Yes, sir.

EIGHT:
CU CROCKER, in the hall, closing the door. His expression is pure contempt.

NO COPY.

Page 8

ONE:
Interior of the Pit, angle on CHACE at her desk. Her hands are steepled, and she's holding a CIGARETTE between her fingers, watching it burn down. Smoke is wafting.

She looks tired and a little haunted.

NO COPY.

TWO:
POV CHACE, past the smoke from her cigarette, over to KITTERING'S EMPTY DESK.

NO COPY.

THREE:
Angle on CHACE, either staring at the smoke or nothing.

1 CHACE:
>   Tom?

                  2 WALLACE/off:
                                      Hmm?

FOUR:
Angle past WALLACE, who is at his desk, legs up,
a folder against his thighs, reading. He's got a
pen in one hand.

CHACE hasn't moved.

                  3 CHACE:
                                      You ever seen Callard?

                  4 WALLACE:
                                      The Madwoman of the Second Floor?

                  5 WALLACE/linked:
                                      Not for a while, no.

Page 9

ONE:
CU CHACE, profile, as she takes a drag on the
cigarette. Still focused on Kittering's desk,
off.

NO COPY.

TWO:
From KITTERING'S DESK, CHACE still staring.

WALLACE has noticed that she's acting kind of
off, and is straightening at his desk, feet back
on the floor.

                  1 WALLACE:
                                      Coming up on FOUR years, in fact.

THREE:
WALLACE, brow creasing as he leans forward.
Concern.

                  2 WALLACE:
                                      You didn't see her after KOSOVO?

FOUR:
CHACE looking at WALLACE as if she's just
remembered they're in the same office. WALLACE
still has the same gentle concern on his face.

                  3 CHACE:
                                      Wasn't TIME.

                  4 CHACE/linked:
                                      Sick LEAVE from the INJURY. Then
                                      this THING with the RUSSIANS.

FIVE:

OTS WALLACE, CHACE looking at him. Expression is
much the same. The burning cigarette between her
fingers. It's like she's looking at him, but not
seeing him. A Thousand Yard Stare.

5 WALLACE:
                    You should make an APPOINTMENT.

SIX:
ECU CHACE'S fingers as she crushes out the
cigarette in the empty, stained, glass ashtray on
her desk.

6 CHACE/above:
                    I'm fine, Tom.[6]

6. For a secret agent, she's not a terribly
convincing liar, here.

Page 10

ONE:
Interior, the ante-room to Crocker's office.
KATE is refilling the coffeemaker. The door into
Crocker's office is open, and CROCKER is visible at
his desk, suit jacket off, examining some eight-
by-tens.

The door from the hall has just been slammed open,
and WELDON is barreling into the space.

1 KATE:
                    …make this and then I'm OFF.

2 CROCKER:
                    Who said you could GO?

3 KATE:
                    It's twenty past SIX on a FRIDAY,
                    Paul—

4 WELDON:
                    WHERE IS HE?

TWO:
OTS CROCKER, looking up as WELDON fills his
doorway.

KATE is just past WELDON'S shoulder.

5 KATE:
                    Deputy Chief to see you, Sir.

6 CROCKER:
                    Hullo, sir.

THREE:
WELDON at CROCKER'S DESK, slamming the FOLDER
from that morning onto the arrayed eight-by-tens.
The eight-by-tens are all satellite surveillance
shots.

7 WELDON:
>   Will you NEVER learn?

8 CROCKER:
>   Can I assume the proposal will go
>   to 'C' WITHOUT your endorsement?

FOUR:
WELDON is frustrated beyond words. CROCKER is
still seated, and he's almost amused.

9 WELDON:
>   It won't go to 'C' at ALL, Paul!

10 WELDON/linked:
>   You will not MOUNT, I will not
>   ENDORSE, and 'C' will not AUTHORIZE
>   an assassination of this KIND.

FIVE:
CROCKER leaning forward slightly, perhaps one
elbow on the desk.

11 CROCKER:
>   What sort of ASSASSINATION will
>   you ENDORSE?

12 CROCKER/linked:
>   Perhaps we can work something out...
>   .

Page 11

ONE:
WELDON fuming at the desk, staring at CROCKER, who
is returning it evenly.

NO COPY.

TWO:
Stet.

1 WELDON:
>   The RUSSIANS are in CUSTODY.

2 WELDON/linked:
>   It's OVER. It's FINISHED.

THREE:
WELDON'S HAND as it takes the FOLDER from
Crocker's DESK.

3 WELDON/off:
>   So you had BEST forget about your
>   VENDETTA...

FOUR:
OTS CROCKER as WELDON goes through the doorway,
back to us. He has the FOLDER in his HAND.

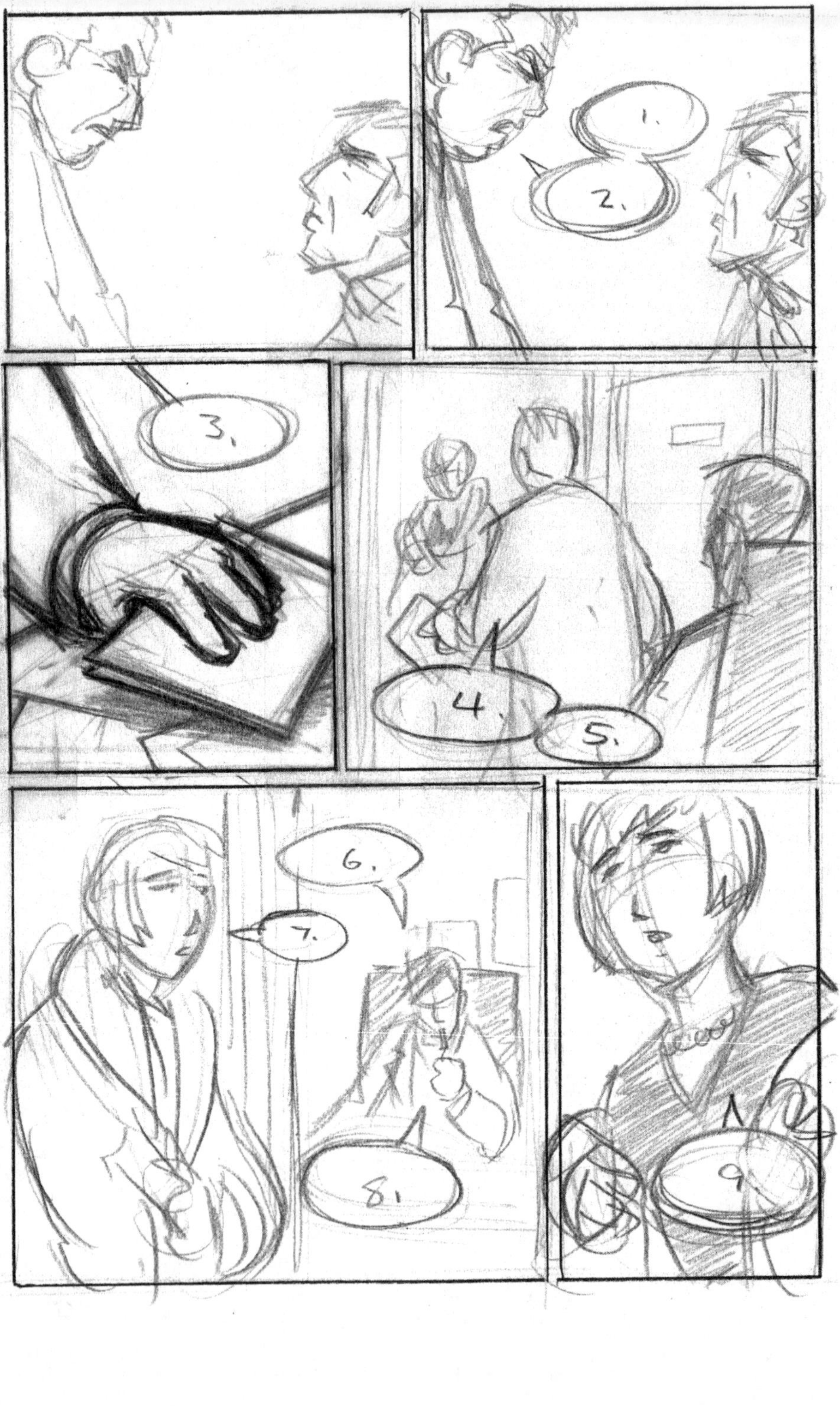
1.
2.
3.
4.
5.
6.
7.
8.
9.

KATE is at her desk in BG, pulling on her coat.

4 WELDON:
>...and turn your ATTENTION to operations ELSEWHERE.

5 WELDON:
>Good evening.

FIVE:
Past KATE, looking at where WELDON has exited the office, the door slamming behind him.

In CROCKER'S office, we can see CROCKER lighting a cigarette.

6 CROCKER:
>He GONE?

7 KATE:
>Yes.

8 CROCKER:
>Then call CHENG. Tell her I need to TALK to her TONIGHT.

SIX:
CU of KATE, almost rolling her eyes, and removing her overcoat.

10 KATE:
>She's dining with a TRADE GROUP at eight....

Page 12

ONE:
Exterior South Kensington street, night. Outside CHACE'S home, as CHACE gets out of her car.

The street is mostly bare, lit by a couple street-lamps. A COUPLE is walking hand-in-hand on the opposite side of the street.

NO COPY.

TWO:
Angle on CHACE as she closes her door, watching the COUPLE. Her expression is tired, almost in blank.

NO COPY.

THREE:
ECU of CHACE'S hand, her keys as she fits them in the lock of her door.

NO COPY.

FOUR:
Interior of the house, the front hall, as CHACE closes the door behind her. With one hand she's pulling the curtains back that cover the window on the side of her front door.

NO COPY.

FIVE:
Very tight, past CHACE, peering through the
gap. The COUPLE is going on their way, utterly
innocent.

NO COPY.

Page 13

ONE:
Tight CU of CHACE'S, maybe upper body, same blank
expression, cigarette burning at her lips.

NO COPY.

TWO:
Interior of the Kitchen, and we're behind CHACE,
and we see that she's standing in front of
her REFRIGERATOR, staring at the almost empty
shelves.

NO COPY.

THREE:
Stet.

NO COPY.

FOUR:
Stet angle, but now the REFRIGERATOR is closed,
and CHACE has turned, reaching to a cabinet where
she is pulling down a BOTTLE OF SCOTCH and a
GLASS.

NO COPY.

FIVE:
From behind, framed in an interior doorway, CHACE
walking away from us, BOTTLE in one hand, GLASS in
the other, cigarette still burning.

NO COPY.

ONE:
Exterior London Street, night, outside of a Very Nice Restaurant.

PEDESTRIANS move back and forth, some well-dressed, some quite casual.

CROCKER is leaning against a wall, still in his three-piece suit, eating FISH and CHIPS from a wrapper.

NO COPY.

TWO:
Angle past CROCKER, who is apparently quite interested in his FISH AND CHIPS, as CHENG comes out of a restaurant behind him. CHENG is looking quite elegant, wearing a very nice dress with a wrap.

NO COPY.

THREE:
CROCKER turning to see her as she approaches. CHENG is scowling.

1 CHENG:
    Kate made it sound like the WORLD was ENDING.

2 CHENG/linked:
    Is the world ENDING?

3 CROCKER:
    I need a FAVOR.

4 CROCKER/linked:
    Chip?

FOUR:
CHENG and CROCKER walking down the street. CHENG is making a face and pulling her head back as if the FISH AND CHIPS smell revolting.

5 CHENG:
    I was in the middle of a veal escalope and YOU offer me a piece of FRIED potato.

6 CROCKER:
    Wish I could do BETTER. On my WAGE, I can hardly AFFORD to SAY 'veal escalope.'

FIVE:
Wide angle as CHENG and CROCKER turn a corner,
basically planning on walking around the block.

7 CHENG:
> My CUP of PITY is OVERFLOWING.

8 CHENG/linked:
> What do you need that can't WAIT
> until tomorrow?

9 CROCKER:
> I think FIVE is going to LOSE the
> RUSSIANS.

Page 15

ONE:
CHENG adjusting her wrap, CROCKER walking
alongside, eating.

1 CHENG/small:
> Dammit it's COLD.

2 CHENG/linked:
> Lose them HOW?

3 CROCKER:
> Not sure. But Weldon was talking
> about EXTRADITION to MOSCOW.

TWO:
From the side, CHENG almost shrugging. CROCKER is
looking off to a side.

4 CROCKER:
> I spoke with Rayburn[7], and he's
> heard rumors that there's a DEAL
> already in PLACE.

5 CROCKER/linked:
> Doesn't know with WHOM.

6 CHENG:
> D. Int hears a rumor and therefore
> you ruin my dinner.

7 CHENG/linked:
> Let it GO, Paul, let it be someone
> else's PROBLEM for

ONCE.

THREE:
CROCKER dropping his FISH AND CHIPS into a
trashcan.

CHENG is alongside, watching the street.

7. I believe this is the first reference to Crocker's opposite number within SIS, Simon Rayburn, the Director of Intelligence (D-Int). Simon's one of those characters who has yet to really break out of the background of series, which is a pity, since he's a neat guy and I'd like to show more of him. One of the drawbacks in writing a 24 page comic book.

8 CROCKER:

It's not what I WANT.

9 CROCKER/linked:

I tried to get OFFICIAL sanction, but WELDON stopped me before I even had my BOOTS on.

FOUR:

CROCKER moving forward, towards us, CHENG still past him, not moving, watching. Not happy.

10 CROCKER:

They're at the FARM now, but it won't be for much longer. No idea where they'll be moved next. No idea when.

11 CHENG:

Paul, why are you telling me this? What do you WANT?

FIVE:

OTS CHENG, CROCKER giving her a look that pretty much says, if you have to ask, you're dumb, and you're not dumb, so why are you even asking.

NO COPY.

SIX:

CU CHENG, sighing.

13 CHENG:

Fine.

14 CHENG/linked:

But remember, YOU asked ME.

Page 16

ONE:
Exterior of MI-6, morning, bright and shiny.

1 'C'/inside:
>...to address Donald's CONCERNS.

TWO:
Interior of C's office, with CROCKER standing by
C's desk as 'C' comes around the side, holding up
the FOLDER from page 11.

2 'C':
>This is an ALARMING proposal,
>Paul.

3 CROCKER:
>It SHOULD be, sir.

4 CROCKER/linked:
>The purpose of that operation is
>to put the FEAR of GOD into ANY
>group that would HUNT and KILL our
>agents.

THREE:
Angle on the desk, as 'C' slaps the FOLDER back
down.

5 'C':
>It goes TOO far.

FOUR:
CROCKER, evenly, and verging on disrespectful.
'C' is turning from the desk to face him again,
and is mildly alarmed by Crocker's tone.

6 CROCKER:
>I DISAGREE, sir. It doesn't go far
ENOUGH.

7 'C':
>I BEG your pardon?

8 CROCKER:
>We were ATTACKED in our HOME.

9 CROCKER/linked:
>They put a BOUNTY on the HEAD of Minder
Two.

FIVE:
OTS 'C', CROCKER is passionate. He's not yelling,
but he absolutely believes in his job, and to him,
the situation is intolerable. This, incidentally,
is why Crocker downs about three gallons of Maalox
a week.

10 CROCKER:

>>>>We are HMG's SECRET INTELLIGENCE SERVICE, yetthese HOODS attempted to TERRORIZE us.

11 CROCKER/linked:

>>>>We MUST strike BACK, sir.

SIX:
CU CROCKER, emphatic.

12 CROCKER:

>>>>We owe it to CHACE, and to ALL of our agents.

13 CROCKER/linked:

>>>>Not just for what we've asked of them, but for what we MAY ask of them.

SEVEN:
CROCKER, turning away slightly, almost embarrassed.

14 CROCKER:
>>>>Unless our agents KNOW we will fight for them, how can we ask them to give their lives for US?
15 CROCKER:

>>>>We MUST strike back.

Page 17

ONE:
Past CROCKER, still looking away from 'C.' For his part, 'C' has his hands deep in his pockets, his chin on his chest, deep in thought.

NO COPY.

TWO:
Angle, 'C' looking at CROCKER.

1 'C':

>>>>Even KNOWING this government's policy on ASSASSINATION, you proposed this operation ANYWAY.

THREE:
Past CROCKER, watching as 'C' comes back around the desk, returning to his seat.

2 'C':

>>>>I don't know if that SPEAKS of you WELL, or as a FOOL.

3 CROCKER:

>>>>We HAVE to PUNISH—

3 'C':
> They ARE being PUNISHED, Paul.

FOUR:
Two-shot, 'C' leaning forward at his desk, CROCKER stiff as a rod.

4 CROCKER:
> The FARM isn't really HARD TIME, though, is it?

5 'C':
> The FARM is not the end of their JOURNEY.

FIVE:
CROCKER reacting, trying to cover his alarm.

6 CROCKER:
> Then they ARE going back to Russia?

SIX:
OTS CROCKER, 'C' looking at him levelly.

7 'C':
> Don't EVEN consider it, Paul.

8 'C'/linked:
> There are OTHER things at stake here besides your OVER-DEVELOPED sense of DOMINION.

SEVEN:
CROCKER turning to go.

'C' returning to his work on the desk.

9 'C':
> And I told you ALREADY, you're REPLACEABLE.

Page 18

ONE:
Exterior of Hyde Park, day. Sunny and bright and lovely, and people are wandering around, doing their things.

In the center of our shot sits ANGELA CHENG at a bench, sunglasses on, looking at the world as it goes by.

She has a NEWSPAPER on her lap.

NO COPY.

TWO:
Stet. Pedestrians continue to move to and fro.

CROCKER is approaching the bench.

1 TAILLESS/elec:
>P.A to D. Ops.

2 TAILLESS/elec:
>Kate, it's D. Ops. How many Minders are in the Pit?

THREE:
Stet. CROCKER is now seated at the bench with CHENG, the paper between them.

3 TAILLESS/elec:
>You've got the complete set.

4 TAILLESS/elec:
>Get them into the Ops Room QUIETLY. I'll BRIEF them when I get back.

FOUR:
Stet. CHENG is gone.

5 TAILLESS/elec:
>By quietly you mean 'without Weldon finding out'?

6 TAILLESS/elec:
>Just do it, Kate.

FIVE:
Stet, and the bench is empty. The NEWSPAPER is gone.

7 TAILLESS/elec:
>Of course, sir.

Page 19

ONE:
Interior of the OPS ROOM. RON is at his desk eating a sandwich.

KITTERING is flirting with ALEXIS.

CHACE is seated at the briefing desk, with WALLACE. Both are smoking.

CROCKER is entering, carrying a rolled up map.

1 CROCKER:
>Ed, if you can stop MOLESTING Lex for a few minutes, I'd APPRECIATE your ATTENTION.

TWO:
At the Briefing Desk, WALLACE and CHACE are watching KITTERING, as KITTERING hurries to take

a seat.

CROCKER stands over them, impatient.

2 KITTERING:

> It was NOTHING, boss. Totally
> INNOCENT.

3 CROCKER:

> If Lex is INNOCENT, I'm your
> mother.

4 CROCKER:

> They're moving the Russians off
> the Farm TONIGHT.

5 CROCKER/linked:

> If it's going to be DONE, it's got
> to be done THEN.

THREE:
Around the table, CHACE, WALLACE, and KITTERING
listening closely as CROCKER explains.

6 CROCKER:

> If any of you has TROUBLE with
> this, say it NOW.

7 KITTERING:

> No, sir.

8 WALLACE:

> You didn't get CLEARANCE, did
> you?

FOUR:
Past CROCKER, not glaring, but honestly not
wanting the debate with WALLACE. WALLACE isn't
looking for a fight either, but he's genuinely not
happy to know this is unauthorized.

9 CROCKER:

> No, I didn't. You're free to go if
> you'd rather, Tom.

10 WALLACE:

> I'm not going anywhere.

11 CROCKER:

> Glad to hear it.

FIVE:
OTS CROCKER, unrolling a roadmap onto the table.

12 CROCKER:

> It needs to look like an
> ACCIDENT...

Page 20

[*Steve-We're going for a sense of serious time passage here, and I'm not sure the best way to highlight that. Perhaps with an underlying image, or simply by having some of the panels bleed off the page. Whatever works best—GR*]

ONE:
Exterior, the 158 in the Cotswolds, night. An utterly average and mundane looking CAR is parked just off the road, beneath the trees, it's lights off. CHACE is behind the wheel, fighting to stay awake. She wears the jacket from the beginning of the issue.

NO COPY.

TWO:
Outside CHACE'S car, and in EBG on the other side of the road, we can see ANOTHER CAR, also parked and partially hidden.

NO COPY.

THREE:
Interior of the OTHER CAR, and we can see KITTERING behind the wheel. Past him, in the EBG, we can see the back of TARA'S PARKED CAR.

NO COPY.

FOUR:
Angle on the TWO CARS. Dark, quiet night.

Nothing is happening.

A leaf blows by.

NO COPY.

Page 21

ONE:
Interior of Crocker's home, the front hallway. This is a fairly nice house outside of London.

CROCKER is coming down the hall in a bathrobe, switching on the light. He's clearly just woken up.

NO COPY.

TWO:
OTS CROCKER, opening the front door to see CHACE, with KITTERING right behind her. Their CARS are visible, parked in the BG.

Again, establish that CHACE is wearing the jacket from the beginning of the issue, with the same bullet-hole in its shoulder.

It's just before dawn, now.

1 CHACE:
> We've been HAD.

THREE:
Reverse, OTS CHACE of CROCKER in the doorway, leaning against the doorframe and rubbing at his eyes.

2 CROCKER:
> They didn't SHOW?

FOUR:
View of CHACE and KITTERING, CROCKER in the doorway. CROCKER is practically scowling, his mind racing.

3 KITTERING:
> NO one SHOWED.

4 CHACE:
> Wallace RADIOED from outside the FARM, says the WHOLE place is shut TIGHT.

FIVE:
Angle in the hallway, CROCKER turning. CHACE and KITTERING visible through the doorway.

5 CROCKER:
> Let me get DRESSED.

6 CROCKER/linked:
> Ed, head back to the OFFICE. Tara, you STAY.

7 CHACE:
> Do I get to COME inside, then?

SIX:
Angle past CHACE, watching as CROCKER ascends the stairs.

8 CROCKER:
> My WIFE wouldn't APPROVE.[8]

8. Many people read this as a throwaway, but Crocker's wife, Jenny, actually does make an appearance in the first Declassified series, as well as the novel. I wanted a contrast; where we've seen Chace alone and isolated, returning to an empty flat with a bottle of scotch for company, here we have Crocker, still cranky, still generally unpleasant, but at least somehow maintaining a home life. I also wanted to humanize Crocker's zealotry. For all he says and does, he's happily married, and at the end of the day, he has a home and a family waiting for him.

Page 22

ONE:
Exterior of an AIRFIELD outside of London. Dawn is starting to break.

We're looking through the gate at CHACE'S car, which has pulled to a stop on the side of the road. CROCKER is emerging from one side, CHACE from behind the wheel.

1 CROCKER:
You have OPTICS?

2 CHACE:
Binoculars in the boot.

3 CROCKER:
Bring them.

TWO:
CHACE and CROCKER, almost side-by-side, at the fence. This is pretty tight on them. CROCKER is raising the BINOCULARS.

NO COPY.

THREE:
CROCKER'S POV, view of the TWO RUSSIANS being escorted onto the parked JET on the airfield.

NO COPY.

FOUR:
CROCKER'S POV, and the view has slid along the fuselage of the plane, to the tail, where a small AMERICAN FLAG has been painted.

NO COPY.

FIVE:
CU CROCKER, lowering the binoculars.

Angry.

3 CROCKER:
Bastards.

Page 23

ONE:
Angle past CHACE, of CROCKER, now by the gate as a string of CARS passes. ONE has pulled to a side, stopping.

NO COPY.

TWO:
CHACE by the passenger door, CROCKER in front of it. The door has opened, and CHENG is getting out.

We can see that there is ANOTHER PASSENGER in the car.

1 CHENG:
> Paul.

2 CHENG/linked:
> They'd ALREADY arranged the DEAL with FIVE—

3 CROCKER:
> You're BLOODY CIA in LONDON, Angela!

4 CROCKER/linked:
> You should have told Langley to FUCK OFF.

THREE:
Angle past CHACE, looking into the back of the car. CHENG and CROCKER moving into BG, arguing.

5 CHENG:
> I'm trying to TELL you it WASN'T the Company that DID this!

FOUR:
OTS CHACE looking into the car, where we see KINNEY seated, looking at her. He looks pretty smug.

6 CHENG/off:
> Kinney went to the FBI before the Russians were even in CUSTODY.

FIVE:
POV KINNEY, of CHACE, just looking at him. It's that same almost blank look she's been cultivating all throughout the book so far. It's a look that says she knows eleven different ways to kill him right now, and if she's bored enough, she might try them all.

The BULLET HOLE is still evident in the shoulder of her jacket.

In EBG, we can see CHENG and CROCKER still going at it.

7 CHENG:
> I didn't find OUT until I went to do you a FAVOR yesterday.

8 CROCKER:
> You should have warned me OFF.

SIX:
Stet, a little tighter. CHACE is removing her
jacket, but she's not looking away from Kinney,
off.

9 TAILLESS/small:
                    …a BREAK…NOT going to SCREW the
                    FBI—

10 TAILLESS/small:
                    —screw US instead…

SEVEN:
Stet, even tighter, and CHACE has just the tiniest
hint of a smile. Jacket is off.

11 TAILLESS/small:
                    …BASTARD tried to get my agent
                    KILLED….

12 CHACE/small:
                    WORD of advice for you, Mister
                    Kinney…

Page 24

ONE:
OTS CHACE, leaning in, jacket bunched in one
hand.

KINNEY in the backseat is fairly intimidated, but
trying to hide it.

1 CHACE:
                    …next time you find someone SHOOTING
                    at YOU…

TWO:
Angle on the seat and perhaps KINNEY'S thigh, as
Chace's JACKET lands. BULLET HOLE visible.

2 CHACE/off:
                    …and you're UNARMED…

THREE:
POV KINNEY, of CHACE crouched just outside the
car, as before. Her expression has changed, is
almost innocently sweet. She's cocked her head
slightly to a side, as if trying to imagine the
scenario.

3 CHACE:
                    …run AT the shooter.

4 CHACE/linked:
                    It throws off their AIM, you see.

FOUR:
Almost stet, but this is now a CU of CHACE, and

her smile is anything but sweet, and her eyes are very angry.

5 CHACE:
                    If you're very lucky.

FIVE:
From above the car, angle, CHACE walking away.

In BG CROCKER and CHENG are still arguing silently.

NO COPY.

SIX:
On CHACE, coming towards us. She looks emotionally wrecked, just drained—a far cry from the act she was giving Kinney.

CROCKER and CHENG still arguing in the BG.

NO COPY.

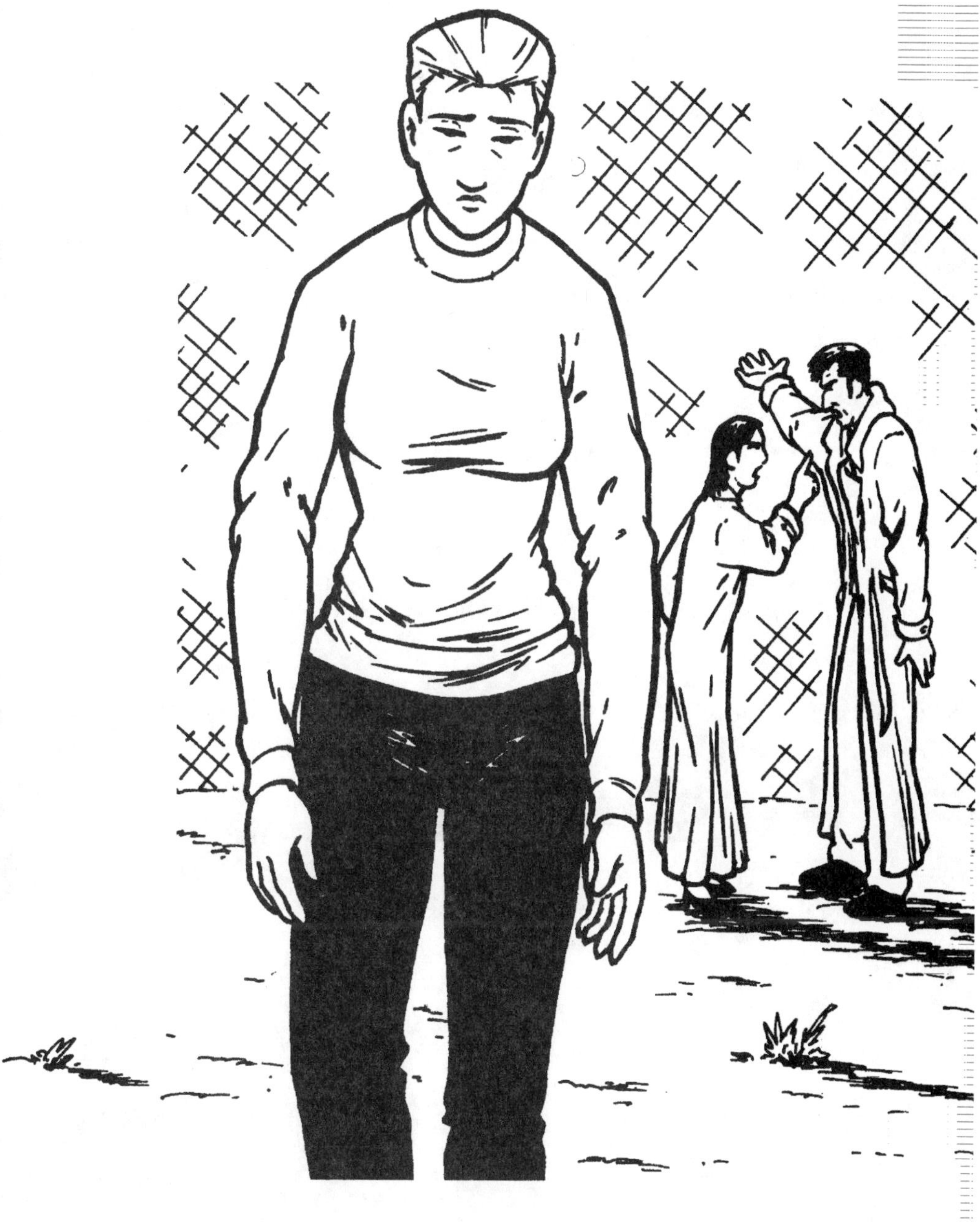

Greg Rucka
www.gregrucka.com

Born in San Francisco, Greg Rucka
was raised on the Monterey Peninsula.
He is the author of several novels,
including four about bodyguard Atticus
Kodiak, and several comic books, for
which he has won two Eisner Awards. He
resides in Portland, Oregon, with his
wife, Jennifer, and their children,
Elliot and Dashiell.